Process Writing Mini-Lessons for Differentiated Writing Instruction

Table of Contents

Introduction ii

Aligning *Benchmark Advance* and *Units of Study* iii

Unit 2, Week 3
Opinion **2**

Unit 3, Week 3
Informative/Explanatory **12**

Unit 4, Week 3
Narrative **22**

Unit 5, Week 3
Opinion **32**

Unit 6, Weeks 2–3
Narrative **42**

Unit 7, Weeks 2–3
Informative/Explanatory **62**

Unit 8, Weeks 2–3
Opinion **82**

Unit 9, Weeks 2–3
Informative/Explanatory **102**

Unit 10, Weeks 2–3
Poetry: Acrostics **122**

Writing Reflection **132**

Blackline Masters **142**

Introduction

The daily writing mini-lessons in the Grade 1 Benchmark Advance Teacher's Resource System enable teachers to seamlessly integrate reading and writing instruction. Each day's writing mini-lesson builds directly upon what students have focused on in their reading mini-lessons.

The Grade 1 *Benchmark Advance Process Writing Handbook* provides alternative instruction that teachers may use to provide more extended and rigorous writing instruction within each unit. For units 2–5, there are mini-lessons to support 5-day process writing experiences, and in units 6–9 the mini-lessons support 10-day process writing experiences. Unit 10 provides both a 5-day process writing for poetry and a week of reflection. These mini-lessons allow teachers to model specific steps in the writing process and support students to independently write their own narrative, informative/explanatory, and opinion texts.

The daily instruction for each process writing experience includes:

– 10-minute focused mini-lesson

– Differentiated conferring prompts to support students during independent writing time

– Quick partner or group-share activities at the end of writing time

– 5-minute "Build Language" grammar mini-lessons to use as needed

The chart below shows how to fit the process writing mini-lessons into each unit.

Unit	Topic	Week 1	Week 2	Week 3
1	Government and Citizenship	Daily Writing to Sources (Narrative, Informative, and Opinion Tasks)		
2	Character	Daily Writing to Sources		5-Day Process Writing: Opinion
3	Life Science	Daily Writing to Sources		5-Day Process Writing: Informative/Explanatory
4	Point of View	Daily Writing to Sources		5-Day Process Writing: Narrative
5	Technology and Science	Daily Writing to Sources		5-Day Process Writing: Opinion
6	Theme	Daily Writing to Sources	10-Day Process Writing: Personal Narratives	
7	History and Culture	Daily Writing to Sources	10-Day Process Writing: Informative Texts	
8	Earth Science	Daily Writing to Sources	10-Day Process Writing: Opinion	
9	Economics	Daily Writing to Sources	10-Day Process Writing: Informative Texts	
10	Physical Science	Daily Writing to Sources	5-Day Poetry Process Writing: Acrostics (Week 2)	Reflection Week

Aligning *Benchmark Advance* and *Units of Study*

For teachers who are currently implementing the Grade 1 Units of Study for Teaching Writing and would like to continue using these units with Benchmark Advance, the following chart provides a suggested alignment that maximizes the connections teachers can make between the Benchmark Advance topics and reading selections and corresponding *Units of Study*.

Unit	Topic	Benchmark Advance Writing			Suggested TCRWP Units of Study
		Week 1	**Week 2**	**Week 3**	
1	Government and Citizenship	Daily Writing to Sources			Small Moments: Writing with Focus, Detail, and Dialogue (Book 1)
2	Character	Daily Writing to Sources		Process Writing: Opinion	Writing Reviews (Book 3)
3	Life Science	Daily Writing to Sources		Process Writing: Informative/ Explanatory	
4	Point of View	Daily Writing to Sources		Process Writing: Narrative	From Scenes to Series: Writing Fiction (Book 4)
5	Technology and Science	Daily Writing to Sources		Process Writing: Opinion	
6	Theme	Daily Writing to Sources	Process Writing: Personal Narratives		Nonfiction Chapter Books (Book 2)
7	History and Culture	Daily Writing to Sources	Process Writing: Informative/ Explanatory		
8	Earth Science	Daily Writing to Sources	Process Writing: Opinion		Writing Like Scientists
9	Economics	Daily Writing to Sources	Process Writing: Informative/ Explanatory		Writing How-To Books
10	Physical Science	Daily Writing to Sources	Process Writing: Poetry (Acrostics)	Reflection Week	Poetry and Songs (If... Then... or 2003 UoS)

The Gingerbread Man

I will be able to:
• Write an opinion statement.
• Use articles in statements about a story.

Additional Materials

Presentation BLM 1
• Opinion Chart

 Handwriting Practice

Model how to write *Gingerbread Man*. Point out the differences in the uppercase **G** and lowercase **g** in the character's name. Make practice pages available in a handwriting center during small-group rotations.

Write Opinion Text: State an Opinion (10 MIN.) RF.1.1a, W.1.1, L.1.1h

Engage Thinking

Explain to students that this week they will follow the steps in the writing process to write an opinion piece. Tell them that they will work on the same piece of writing all week. First, they will state an opinion or how they feel about something. Next, they will give reasons or examples from the text to support their opinion. Then they will write a first draft, and finally they will make their writing better before they share it with others.

Say: *This week, we're going to write an opinion about a character from one of the books we have read. We will follow the steps in the writing process to write the opinion. First we will state an opinion about our favorite character.*

Model

Remind students that when they state an opinion, they tell how they feel or what they think. Tell students that people may have different opinions about the same topic.

Create a two-column chart like the one below. Select one story for modeling and lead students in brainstorming the names of the characters. This model focuses on *The Gingerbread Man*. Record the characters in the left column of the chart.

Characters	I like this character because . . .
little old man	
little old woman	
the Gingerbread Man	
the fox	

Sample Opinion Chart

Sample think-aloud: *Let's look back at the story and write the characters' names on the chart. I read through the list and think that I really like the fox the best. That is my opinion. My favorite character is the fox.*

Practice

Invite students to increase the list of characters to include any story they have read in this unit. Then ask them to choose their favorite. Have them share their favorite character with a partner. Ask students to use the sentence frame: *My favorite character is _____.*

Independent Writing

Ask students to write a sentence that states their opinion by naming their favorite story character. They may need to use the sentence frame: *My favorite character is _____.* Use their writing to assess their understanding of how to state an opinion.

Students may write during writer's workshop time or at a writing station during small-group reading time. Independent Writing should occur before the Partner Share. Use the Build Language Review as needed while you confer and monitor.

Confer and Monitor

As students brainstorm independently, support their efforts as needed using prompts like those provided here.

Directive Feedback: *If you have trouble choosing a character, start by picking just one book and look at the illustrations. Find your favorite illustration. What characters do you see? Which character do you like best?*

Self-Monitoring and Reflection: *How did you decide which character to choose?*

Validating and Confirming: *You stated a strong opinion about your favorite character!*

Partner Share

Say: *Now share your opinion statement with a partner.*

Monitor partners as they share their opinion statements.

Build Language Review: Articles (iELD)

Circle the article **the** in your sample writing. Point out that **the** is an article.

Say: *The words **a, an,** and **the** are special describing words called articles. **A** and **an** are used to tell about any person, place, or thing. **The** is used to tell about an exact person, place, or thing.*

Invite students to help you brainstorm sentences about *The Gingerbread Man.* Point out each article and discuss why it is used. For example:

> **The** old woman makes gingerbread.
> She put **a** currant for his nose.
> She made **an** arm on each side of his body.

Oral Language Practice

Display pages 2–3 of *The Gingerbread Man* and have partners identify the articles *(a, the)* in the text. As they find each article, have them tell their partner why it is used.

(iELD) Integrated ELD

Light Support
Review when to use the articles **a, an,** and **the** with students. Provide sentence frames to review details from *The Gingerbread Man.*
The woman wears _____ apron.
The woman put _____ head on the Gingerbread Man.
The Gingerbread Man ran from _____ little old man.
The Gingerbread rode on _____ fox.

Moderate Support
Remind students to use **an** when a noun or a describing word begins with a vowel. Provide sentence frames to review details from *The Gingerbread Man.*
The woman wears _____ dress. (**an** orange)
The woman put _____ on the Gingerbread Man. (**a** nose; **an** eye; **a** mouth)
The Gingerbread Man ran from _____. (**the** man and woman; **a** boy and **a** girl; **a** dog; **a** cat)
The Gingerbread rode on _____. (**a** fox)

Substantial Support
Remind students to use **an** when a noun or a describing word begins with a vowel. Have students complete sentences with **a** or **an** and read them aloud.
The woman wears _____ orange dress.
The woman put _____ eye on the Gingerbread Man.
The Gingerbread Man ran from _____ cat.
The Gingerbread Man rode on _____ fox.

RF.1.1a Recognize the distinguishing features of a sentence (e.g., first word, capitalization, ending punctuation). **W.1.1** Write opinion pieces in which they introduce the topic or name the book they are writing about, state an opinion, supply a reason for the opinion, and provide some sense of closure. **L.1.1h** Use determiners (e.g., articles, demonstratives).

The Gingerbread Man

Student Objectives

I will be able to:
• Write a reason to support an opinion.
• Use articles and demonstratives in statements about story characters.

Handwriting Practice

Model how to write the straight line letters **I, l, i, k** from the phrase **I like.** Point out how each letter is started with a straight up-and-down line. Make practice pages available in a handwriting center during small-group rotations.

Write Opinion Text: Give Your Reason(s) (10 MIN.) RF.1.1a, W.1.1, L.1.1h

Engage Thinking

Display the two-column Opinion Chart from Day 1.

Say: *Yesterday, we made a chart with the names of the characters. Then we each stated an opinion about which character is our favorite. When you state an opinion, you need to give reasons to support it. Today, we will continue working on our opinion pieces by adding reasons.*

Model (iELD)

Display *The Gingerbread Man* to model how to give reasons that support an opinion. Lead students in completing the sentence frame *I like this character because _____.* Record the reasons in the right column of the chart.

Characters	I like this character because . . .
little old man	he helps the little old woman
little old woman	she bakes good things
the Gingerbread Man	he does whatever he wants
the fox	he is smart and tricks the Gingerbread Man

Sample Opinion Chart

Sample think-aloud: *Let's look back at our story and the reasons we like each character. I think about the sentence I wrote, "My favorite character is the fox." I think about what happens in the story that makes me like the fox. I like the fox because he is smart. He tricks the Gingerbread Man.*

Practice

Invite partners to read aloud their opinion statements to each other. Then have them tell the reason(s) they like that character the best. Encourage them to use the sentence frame *I like _____ because _____.*

Independent Writing

Ask students to write a sentence or two that gives the reason(s) they like the character they chose as their favorite. They may need to use the sentence frame *I like _____ because _____.* Use their writing to assess their understanding of how to give a reason.

Students may write during writer's workshop time or at a writing station during small-group reading time. Independent Writing should occur before the Partner Share. Use the Build Language Review as needed while you confer and monitor.

Confer and Monitor

As students brainstorm independently, support their efforts as needed using prompts like those provided here.

Directive Feedback: *Look back at the parts of the story that tell about your character's actions. Retell something the character did that you like.*

Self-Monitoring and Reflection: *How is the character you chose different from other characters you read about? How is the character important in the story?*

Validating and Confirming: *Excellent! That's a good reason to like that character.*

Partner Share

Say: *Now share your reason or reasons with a partner.*

Monitor partners as they share their reason(s).

Build Language Review: Articles and Demonstratives

Remind students that **a, an,** and **the** are special describing words called articles. Remind them that **that, this, these,** and **those** are special describing words called demonstratives.

Say: *Remember that we use the article **an** before words that begin with vowels **a, e, i, o, u,** and we use the article **a** before words that begin with consonants. Remember that we use the demonstratives **this** and **that** with singular nouns and **these** and **those** with plural nouns.*

Display the following sentences. Underline each article and demonstrative. Ask students to identify the noun or describing word each article or demonstrative describes and why that article or demonstrative is used.

> She uses <u>a</u> raisin for an eye.
> She uses <u>these</u> cherries for buttons.
> "I'll use this currant for <u>a</u> nose," said the little old woman.
> <u>That</u> Gingerbread Man runs fast!

Oral Partner Practice

Invite partners to use the articles **a, an,** and **the** and the demonstratives **that, this, these,** and **those** to tell facts about their favorite characters.

RF.1.1a Recognize the distinguishing features of a sentence (e.g., first word, capitalization, ending punctuation). **W.1.1** Write opinion pieces in which they introduce the topic or name the book they are writing about, state an opinion, supply a reason for the opinion, and provide some sense of closure. **L.1.1h** Use determiners (e.g., articles, demonstratives).

Write Opinion Text: Draft (10 MIN.)

RF.1.1a, W.1.1, L.1.1c, L.1.6

The Gingerbread Man

Student Objectives

I will be able to:
• Write a draft of an opinion piece.
• Make sentences using singular and plural nouns with matching verbs.

Additional Materials

Presentation BLM 2
• Singular and Plural Nouns and Matching Verbs Chart

Handwriting Practice

Model how to write the word **because**. Point out how to make the curved letters **b, e, c, a, u**, and **s**. Make practice pages available in a handwriting center during small-group rotations.

Engage Thinking

Display the Opinion Chart.

Say: *We each chose a favorite character and stated an opinion. Then we each wrote the reasons for our opinion. Today we will put it all together. We will combine the opinion and reasons into one piece of writing. This writing is a draft. I am going to show you how I write a draft for an opinion, then you will draft your own.*

Model

Think aloud as you draft an opinion piece. For example:

• *I'm going to state my opinion in the first sentence. What sentence frame did we use to state an opinion about a character? That's right:* My favorite character is the fox.
• *Next I need to add the reasons that support my opinion. What reasons did I give on the chart? I will write those next.*
• *Because I am writing about specific characters, I use the article* **the** *in front of the nouns* **fox** *and* **Gingerbread Man.**
• *This is a good start and I will have a chance to make it even better tomorrow. Let's all read what I've written.*

Sample Draft

My favorite character is the fox. I like the fox because he is a smart fox. He tricks the Gingerbread Man.

Practice

Invite partners to read their opinion and reason(s) to one another several times. Explain that writers often read a sentence out loud to see how it sounds.

Independent Writing

Say: *Now it's your turn to write your draft of an opinion piece. Do your best! But remember that this is a draft, so you'll have a chance to make your writing better tomorrow.*

Students may write during writer's workshop time or at a writing station during small-group reading time. Independent Writing should occur before the Partner Share. Use the Build Language Review as needed while you confer and monitor.

 **Confer and Monitor**

As students brainstorm independently, support their efforts as needed using prompts like those provided here.

Directive Feedback: *Remember to start your draft by stating your opinion:* My favorite character is _____. *Then tell why you like the character:* I like _____ because _____.

Self-Monitoring and Reflection: *Show me where you stated your opinion. Now show me the reasons you have given to support that opinion.*

Validating and Confirming: *You began by stating an opinion. Your reasons clearly support that opinion.*

Partner Share

Say: *Now share your writing with a partner. Read your opinion and reasons aloud to your partner. Talk about ways you might make the writing better tomorrow.*

Monitor partners as they share their writing.

Build Language Review: Singular and Plural Nouns with Matching Verbs (iELD)

Remind students that the verbs in their sentences should match the nouns. Remind them that a singular noun names one person, place, or thing, and a plural noun names more than one person, place, or thing.

Say: *A verb that matches a singular noun needs an **s** at the end. A verb that matches a plural noun does not need an **s.***

Display the following sentences and ask students to suggest one or more matching verbs for each.

> The Gingerbread Man _____ through the countryside.
> The two animals _____ the Gingerbread Man.
> The fox _____.

Oral Language Practice

Have students turn to a partner. Partners should takes turns making up sentences about their favorite character that include singular nouns with matching verbs, and sentences about the illustrations that include plural nouns and matching verbs.

(iELD) Integrated ELD

Light Support
Have students read and complete the following sentences with the correct form of the verb.
Verb: like
Sentence: *[Student's name] _____ [character's name] the best.*
Verb: make
Sentence: *Stories _____ me want to read more.*
Then have students compose sentences, using singular and plural nouns about their favorite character from this week's reading.

Moderate Support
Invite students to write and read the correct form of the verb.
Verb: like
Sentence: *[Student's name] _____ [character's name] the best.*
Verb: make
Sentence: *Stories _____ me feel good.*
Have students write and read a sentence, using their favorite character's name (singular noun) and then one using plural objects from that character's story.

Substantial Support
Invite students to write and read the correct form of the verb.
Verb: like
Sentence: *[Student's name] _____ [character's name] the best.*
Verb: make
Sentence: *Stories _____ me smile.*
Have students tell a sentence using their favorite character's name (singular noun) and then one using plural objects from that character's story.

RF.1.1a Recognize the distinguishing features of a sentence (e.g., first word, capitalization, ending punctuation). **W.1.1** Write opinion pieces in which they introduce the topic or name the book they are writing about, state an opinion, supply a reason for the opinion, and provide some sense of closure. **L.1.1c** Use singular and plural nouns with matching verbs in basic sentences (e.g., He hops; We hop). **L.1.6** Use words and phrases acquired through conversations, reading and being read to, and responding to texts, including using frequently occurring conjunctions to signal simple relationships (e.g., because).

The Gingerbread Man

Student Objectives

I will be able to:
• Revise and edit a draft.
• Use nouns with matching verbs.

Additional Materials

Presentation BLM 3
• Editing Checklist

Handwriting Practice

Model how to write *my favorite*. Point out the tricky formations in the letter **f**, starting at the top of the hook and going down and ending with the cross. Make practice pages available in a handwriting center during small-group rotations.

Write Opinion Text: Revise and Edit

(10 MIN.) **RF.1.1a, W.1.1, W.1.5, L.1.1c**

Engage Thinking

Display the model draft from Day 3.

Say: *This is the first draft of my opinion piece. Now we will revise and edit our drafts to make them stronger.*

Revise and Edit (IELD)

Model

Explain that revising a piece of writing is to go back to your draft and see where you can make it better. Could you make your point clearer? Did you include evidence for your opinions? When you revise, you add or change your writing to make it stronger. Explain that editing a piece of writing is when you go back to fix mistakes you might have made in spelling, grammar, and so on. Use a think-aloud to model how you revised and edited the opinion piece.

> **Sample Modeled Writing**
> My favorite character is the fox from The Gingerbread Man. I like the fox because he is a smart ~~fox~~. He tricks the Gingerbread Man. He talks the Gingerbread Man into walking closer and closer to his mouth!

Sample think-aloud: *I wrote a draft about how the fox is my favorite character. I revised and edited my draft to make it stronger and more interesting to read. First, I made my opening stronger by adding the title of the book that my character is in. Then I added more reasons to help the reader understand why I like the fox. Finally, I got rid of some words that repeated.*

Next, I corrected errors in spelling, grammar, and punctuation. I followed an editing checklist.

Editing	Check
I used pronouns correctly.	✓
I used correct end punctuation for each sentence.	✓
I used singular and plural nouns with matching verbs.	✓
I used the correct articles where they were needed.	✓
I spelled all words correctly.	✓
I capitalized the first letter of the first word in each sentence.	✓

Editing Checklist

Practice

Invite partners to share the changes each of them plans to make to their essays. Each partner should share at least two changes he or she intends to make.

Independent Writing

Say: *Now it's your turn to write. Revise and edit your own draft to make it stronger.*

Students may write during writer's workshop time or at a writing station during small-group reading time. Independent Writing should occur before the Partner Share. Use the Build Language Review as needed while you confer and monitor.

 Confer and Monitor

As students revise and edit independently, support their efforts as needed using prompts like those provided here.

Directive Feedback: *In your opinion piece, you should tell the name of the story that your character is from. Write the title of the story after you state your opinion.*

Self-Monitoring and Reflection: *What are some reasons you could add when you go back and revise?*

Validating and Confirming: *You used some great supporting reasons. I can really understand why you chose this character as your favorite!*

Whole-Group Share

Say: *Now let's share our writing with the group. Read clearly so everyone can understand.*

Build Language Review: Singular and Plural Nouns with Matching Verbs

Say: *What singular and plural nouns did you use in your writing? Let's check that each verb matches the noun.*

Make a chart of the nouns and matching verbs students identify.

Oral Language Practice

Allow each student to choose a verb from the chart and make up a sentence about their favorite character. Then have partners make up a sentence about their two favorite characters that includes the matching verb.

iELD Integrated ELD

Light Support
Have students answer the question: *Which character did you like best? Why?*
Have pairs use the Opinion Chart from Day 2 to generate a sentence. Then have partners take turns reading aloud their sentence.
Ask: *Which character did you not like? Why not?*
Have pairs revise their first sentence to answer the question. Then have partners take turns reading aloud their sentences.
Have students discuss how their two sentences differed.

Moderate Support
Have students read the question: *Which character did you like best? Why?*
Have pairs use the Opinion Chart from Day 2 to complete the sentence frame *I like _____ best because _____.*
Then have partners take turns reading aloud their sentence.
Ask: *Which character did you not like? Why not?*
Have pairs revise their first sentence to follow the sentence frame *I did not like _____ because _____.*
Lead students to see how their sentences were different.

Substantial Support
Display this week's texts. Have students echo-read the question: *Which character did you like best? Why?*
Have pairs use the Opinion Chart from Day 2 to complete the sentence frame *I like _____ best because _____.*
Ask: *Which character did you not like? Why not?*
Help students revise their first sentence to follow the sentence frame *I did not like _____ because _____.*
Have them echo-read their sentences.

RF.1.1a Recognize the distinguishing features of a sentence (e.g., first word, capitalization, ending punctuation). **W.1.1** Write opinion pieces in which they introduce the topic or name the book they are writing about, state an opinion, supply a reason for the opinion, and provide some sense of closure. **W.1.5** With guidance and support from adults, focus on a topic, respond to questions and suggestions from peers, and add details to strengthen writing as needed. **L.1.1c** Use singular and plural nouns with matching verbs in basic sentences (e.g., He hops; We hop).

The Gingerbread Man

Student Objectives

I will be able to:
- Share writing with a partner.
- Compliment a partner's writing.

Write Opinion Text: Share (10 MIN.) RF.1.1a, W.1.1, SL.1.1a

Engage Thinking

Explain to students that they have completed their writing.

Say: *Now we are ready to share our final texts with the class. Part of sharing our writing is giving compliments to our classmates.*

Peer Collaboration Think-Aloud

Display the final version of the sample writing. Use a think-aloud to model giving compliments to a writer.

Sample Modeled Writing

My favorite character is the fox from <u>The Gingerbread Man</u>. I like the fox because he is smart. He tricks the Gingerbread Man. He talks the Gingerbread Man into walking closer and closer to his mouth!

Sample think-aloud: *Giving a compliment means saying something nice about somebody's writing. Good compliments are kind and specific. Being kind means you tell them that they did a good job or that you really liked what they did. I would say to the writer of our writing sample, "I really like your description of the fox." Then I would add something specific that I liked. "It is great that you gave a good example of how smart the fox is."*

Display a student's opinion piece. Read it aloud.

Say: *I'm going to give [student's name] a compliment. I might say, "I think you chose a great reason for picking a favorite character." For a specific compliment, I might say, [compliment a specific element of the student's writing].*

Peer Collaboration: Give a Compliment (iELD)

Say: *Now it is your turn to give a classmate a compliment. Share your writing with a partner. Think of something positive to say and be sure to tell them about something specific that they did well.*

Students may write out their compliments during writer's workshop time or at a writing station during small-group reading time.

Whole-Group Share

Select a few volunteers to share their opinion piece with the class.

Say: *Now let's share our writing with the class. After a student reads their writing aloud, we will take turns giving the writer compliments.*

Monitor the class as students give the writers compliments.

iELD Integrated ELD

Light Support
Discuss what a compliment is. Invite each student to read and compliment another student on their writing. If needed, provide an example. Then ask students to think of one compliment they could say about a student's writing.

Moderate Support
Discuss what a compliment is. Invite each student to read and compliment another student about their writing. If needed, provide sentence frames.
I like how _____.
I notice you _____.
I like _____.

Substantial Support
Explain that a compliment is something nice you say about another person's work. Tell students that the compliment should state something that is true. Model by sharing a compliment about a student's writing, such as *I like how [student's name] drew a picture of the character [he/she] likes best.* Then invite group members to say a compliment about the writing, using the sentence frame: *I like how [student's name] _____.* Continue with each student's writing.

RF.1.1a Recognize the distinguishing features of a sentence (e.g., first word, capitalization, ending punctuation). **W.1.1** Write opinion pieces in which they introduce the topic or name the book they are writing about, state an opinion, supply a reason for the opinion, and provide some sense of closure. **SL.1.1a** Follow agreed-upon rules for discussions (e.g., listening to others with care, speaking one at a time about the topics and texts under discussion).

Write Informational Text: Brainstorm

(10 MIN.) RF.1.1a, W.1.2, W.1.5, L.1.1d

The Ugly Duckling

Student Objectives

I will be able to:
• Brainstorm ideas to write in an informational text.
• Use personal, possessive, and indefinite pronouns in statements about a story.

Additional Materials

Presentation BLMs 4 and 5
• Brainstorming Chart
• Personal Pronouns Chart

Engage Thinking

Remind students that they have followed the steps in the writing process to write a narrative. Explain that writers of informational texts also follow certain steps in the writing process. First, they think of a topic to write about. Next, they plan their writing. Then they write a first draft, and finally, they make their writing better before they share it with others.

Say: *This week, you are going to work on one piece of writing. You are going to write an informational text about a living thing from one of the texts we have read in this unit. Remember, informational texts give readers facts and true details to the reader. Your informational text will explain how that living thing grows and changes.*

Brainstorm

Model

Remind students that the first step in the writing process is brainstorming. Explain that when writers brainstorm, they think up ideas to write about. They let themselves think about many ideas, and they write them all down. Use a think-aloud to model your brainstorming process.

Sample think-aloud: *I am going to think about all of the different living things we have read about that change. Some are plants and some are animals. I will write down all of my ideas. Writing down my ideas is called brainstorming. We read about different living things that change. I will make a chart to list all of the living things.*

Plants	Animals
Oak tree	Butterfly
Apple tree	Frog

Sample Brainstorming Chart

Sample think-aloud: *Now I can choose the idea I will write about for my informational text. I will choose the living thing that interests me the most. I will write about the butterfly.*

Practice

Invite partners to create brainstorming charts of their own. Have each student add one animal or plant to the chart.

Independent Writing

Say: *Now it's your turn to write. Brainstorm your own ideas. Write a list of living things that you could write about for your own informational text. When you are finished, circle the idea you like the best.*

Students may draw and write during writer's workshop time or at a writing station during small-group reading time. Independent Writing should occur before the Partner Share. Use the Build Language Review as needed while you confer and monitor.

Confer and Monitor

As students brainstorm independently, support their efforts as needed using prompts like those provided here.

Directive Feedback: *Think about all the texts we have read. Close your eyes and imagine the plants and animals we have learned about. Now write the names of those plants and animals.*

Self-Monitoring and Reflection: *Remember that we looked at flow charts that show different parts of a life cycle. What animals and plants were shown in those flow charts? Which living thing's life cycle was most interesting to you?*

Validating and Confirming: *You brainstormed several ideas that you could develop!*

Partner Share

Invite students to share one of their ideas with a partner. Instruct them to follow the rules for collaborative conversation by listening to their partner and taking turns.

Build Language Review: Personal, Possessive, and Indefinite Pronouns

Remind students that they have learned how to replace nouns with personal, possessive, and indefinite pronouns.

Say: *Remember that personal pronouns take the place of a person's name in a sentence. Possessive pronouns take the place of a noun and show ownership. Indefinite pronouns are used when the noun is not specific to a person or thing.*

Lead students in completing each sentence with the correct pronoun.

Pronouns	Sentences
Their	The ducks made fun of the ugly duckling. _____ made fun of him.
He	The ducks followed the mother duck. _____ mother kept them safe.
They	The ugly duckling was alone. _____ felt lonely.

Oral Language Practice

Have partners write their own sentences correctly using at least two personal, possessive, and indefinite pronouns. For example: *I went to the store with my dad. Jane is my sister and she is three years old. They invited me to a skating party.*

---

iELD Integrated ELD

Light Support
Support students as they write sentences about the story using the pronouns **I, me, my, they, them, their, anyone,** and **somebody.**
Ask them to use a pronoun instead of specific names of characters. Ask students to check their work and make sure that their pronouns are correct.

Moderate Support
Have student pairs write about an event in the story. Provide a list of phrases they could use.

It took place _____.	The ducklings _____. They _____.
The ugly duckling felt _____.	I enjoyed this event because _____.

Review using pronouns **I** and **they.**

Substantial Support
Say: *We are going to write some sentences about an event from the story, using pronouns.*
Ask: *Where does the event take place?*
It took place/happened _____.
Ask: *Who was there? What did they do?*
The _____ (ducklings) were there. They _____.
The ugly duckling felt _____ because _____.
Say: *They is a pronoun. What does it stand for?*
(Elicit: the ducklings)

RF.1.1a Recognize the distinguishing features of a sentence (e.g., first word, capitalization, ending punctuation). **W.1.2** Write informative/explanatory texts in which they name a topic, supply some facts about the topic, and provide some sense of closure. **W.1.5** With guidance and support from adults, focus on a topic, respond to questions and suggestions from peers, and add details to strengthen writing as needed. **L.1.1d** Use personal, possessive, and indefinite pronouns (e.g., I, me, my; they, them, their; anyone, everything).

Write Informational Text: Plan

(10 MIN.) W.1.2, W.1.5, L.1.1d

The Ugly Duckling

Additional Materials

Presentation BLMs 6 and 7
• Planning Chart
• Personal Pronouns Chart

Engage Thinking

Tell students that now that they have completed brainstorming and picked a topic, they are ready to plan their writing.

Plan

Model

Remind students that when they plan their writing, they decide what information to include in their text. Use a think-aloud to model how to plan an informational text.

Sample think-aloud: *After brainstorming, I chose the topic of butterflies. I know I am going to write about how butterflies change and grow. For this kind of informational text, the best way to organize my ideas is in the order in which they happen. I will think back to the texts and the flowcharts I read. I know that a butterfly goes from an egg to a caterpillar to a pupa, then finally to a butterfly. I am going to write my ideas in that order.*

Stages in the Life Cycle	Facts
Egg	
Caterpillar	
Pupa	
Butterfly	

Sample think-aloud: *Now I will write facts about each stage. I don't need to write complete sentences. I just want to get my ideas written.*

Stages in the Life Cycle	Facts
Egg	• First stage of life • Caterpillar grows inside egg • Egg is laid on a plant
Caterpillar	• Hatches from the egg • Eats a lot • Grows quickly
Pupa	
Butterfly	

Sample Planning Chart

Practice

Invite partners to add to the butterfly plan. Ask partners to contribute their own facts for the Pupa and Butterfly stages on the chart.

Independent Writing

Say: *Now it's your turn to write. Plan your own ideas for your informative text on how a living thing changes.*

Students may draw and write during writer's workshop time or at a writing station during small-group reading time. Independent Writing should occur before the Partner Share. Use the Build Language Review as needed while you confer and monitor.

Confer and Monitor

As students plan independently, support their efforts as needed using prompts like those provided here.

Directive Feedback: *Visualize the steps in your living thing's life cycle. Write them down in order.*

Self-Monitoring and Reflection: *Take a look at your facts that support each stage. Do you think you are ready to draft? Why or why not?*

Validating and Confirming: *You organized your informational text into clear stages and provided facts about each stage!*

Partner Share

Say: *Now let's share our writing with our partners. Read your writing aloud. Point out the details that support each big idea.*

Monitor partners as they share their writing.

Build Language Review: Personal Pronouns (iELD)

Remind students that pronouns are special words that take the place of nouns. Some pronouns refer to specific people or things, but others don't.

Say: *Writers use pronouns to replace nouns so their writing sounds smoother and more natural. When I write about the ugly duckling, I don't always want to use the words **the ugly duckling** to talk about this character. I can use the pronouns **he** and **him** to replace these words because the ugly duckling is a male.*

Lead students in replacing the boldfaced phrases with pronouns.

Pronouns	Sentences
He	The ugly duckling was sad about what happened to **the ugly duckling.**
Him	**The ugly duckling** told what happened to the ugly duckling.
His	**The ugly duckling's** family abandoned him.

Oral Language Practice

Have partners write their own sentences using personal pronouns such as **he**, **she**, **him**, **her**, **his**, and **hers**. For example: *The book belongs to Stella. The book is hers. Max plays guitar. He plays guitar. Francine has a piano. She has a piano.*

iELD Integrated ELD

Light Support
Draw a two-column chart on the board. For example:

Name (noun)	Pronoun

Have students replace the nouns **the ugly duckling, Mom, a boy student, a girl student, the teacher** with pronouns.

Moderate Support
Draw the chart above on the board. As a group, replace the nouns **the ugly duckling, Mom, a boy student, a girl student, the teacher** *with pronouns.* Have student pairs practice replacing nouns with pronouns. Provide sentence frames.
Noun: *The _____ was sad.*
Pronoun: *_____ was sad.*
Noun: *_____ asked, "Who are you?"* (Mom)
Pronoun: *_____ asked, "Who are you?"* (She)

Substantial Support
Create a chart of nouns and pronouns, using student suggestions.

Name (noun)	Pronoun
the ugly duckling	he or him (ugly duckling is a boy)
mother duck	she or her

Have students use pronouns from the chart to practice sentence frames.
Say: *The* **ugly duckling** *was sad. Let's replace the noun with a pronoun.*
_____ was sad. (He)
Say: *The big ducks pecked the* **ugly duckling.** *Let's replace the noun with a pronoun.*
The big ducks pecked _____. (him)

W.1.2 Write informative/explanatory texts in which they name a topic, supply some facts about the topic, and provide some sense of closure. **W.1.5** With guidance and support from adults, focus on a topic, respond to questions and suggestions from peers, and add details to strengthen writing as needed. **L.1.1d** Use personal, possessive, and indefinite pronouns (e.g., I, me, my; they, them, their; anyone, everything).

Write Informational Text: Draft (10 MIN.)

W.1.2, W.1.5, L.1.1c

The Ugly Duckling

Student Objectives

I will be able to:
- Write a draft of an informational text.
- Use nouns with matching verbs in statements about a story.

Additional Materials

Presentation BLM 8
- Singular and Plural Nouns with Matching Verbs Chart

Engage Thinking

Tell students that now that they have completed their planning, it is time to write a draft of their informational text.

Say: *When you write a draft, you follow your plan and write your sentences about the topic you chose. All of your sentences should be about your topic. The draft is your first attempt. As we go through the writing process, you will get a chance to work with what you write and make it better.*

Draft

Model

Display and read aloud your draft. Then use a think-aloud to discuss what you did.

Sample Modeled Writing

The first stage of a butterfly's life is the egg stage. The egg is laid on a plant. The bug hatches. It eats a lot and grows very quickly. The bug changes to a pupa. The pupa can hang from a branch. The butterfly inside grows quickly. The butterfly comes out of the cocoon. It doesn't grow anymore, but it has large wings for flying.

Sample think-aloud: *I used my plan to draft my informational text. The first part of my plan was about the egg stage, so I wrote about that stage first.*

Next I followed my plan and wrote about the caterpillar stage. Then I wrote about the pupa stage. Finally, I wrote about the butterfly stage because that was the last thing in my plan.

I put all of my sentences together in a paragraph about butterflies. I read my paragraph and made sure all of the sentences made sense and were complete.

Practice

Invite partners to discuss the stages of development they will write about. Have partners review each other's stages and note any important stage of development that might have been left out of his or her partner's writing.

Independent Writing

Say: *Now it's your turn to write. Write your own draft using the plan you created.*

Students may write during writer's workshop time or at a writing station during small-group reading time. Independent Writing should occur before the Partner Share. Use the Build Language Review as needed while you confer and monitor.

Confer and Monitor

As students write independently, support their efforts as needed using prompts like those provided here.

Directive Feedback: *Look at your planning chart. What is the first stage you want to write about?*

Self-Monitoring and Reflection: *Did you look at your planning chart? How did it help you?*

Validating and Confirming: *You have made great progress today writing your stages and facts down!*

Partner Share

Say: *Now let's share our writing with our partners. Read your writing aloud. Point out how your draft follows the plan you created.*

Monitor partners as they share their writing.

Build Language Review: Singular and Plural Nouns with Matching Verbs (iELD)

Review that when a noun and verb are written together in a sentence, they must match.

Say: *Singular nouns and their verbs are formed differently from plural nouns and their verbs. It is important that singular nouns and verbs are used together and plural nouns and verbs are used together. Pay attention to the endings of nouns and verbs and notice when to add an **–s.***

Lead students in changing singular nouns and verbs to plural in sentences.

Singular Noun and Verb	Plural Noun and Verb
The duck swims.	
The egg cracks.	
The swan talks.	

Oral Language Practice

Have partners write their own sentences using first singular nouns and verbs and then plural nouns and verbs. For example: *The cat meows. The cats meow. My friend sings. My friends sing. The boy jumps. The boys jump.*

(iELD) Integrated ELD

Light Support
Have students work with a partner. Give student pairs a list of singular and plural nouns and verbs. Have students work together to write sentences with matching nouns and verbs.

Moderate Support
Give students a list of singular and plural nouns and verbs. Give them sentence frames and have them complete the sentence frames using a matching noun or verb.
The dog _____. (barks)
The dogs _____. (bark)
The _____ runs. (girl)
The _____ run. (girls)

Substantial Support
Give students word cards with a noun or a verb written on each card. Have students match singular nouns and verbs and plural nouns and verbs. Have students talk about their matching pairs with a partner.

W.1.2 Write informative/explanatory texts in which they name a topic, supply some facts about the topic, and provide some sense of closure. **W.1.5** With guidance and support from adults, focus on a topic, respond to questions and suggestions from peers, and add details to strengthen writing as needed. **L.1.1c** Use singular and plural nouns with matching verbs in basic sentences (e.g., He hops; We hop).

An Oak Tree Has a Life Cycle & The Ugly Duckling

Student Objectives

I will be able to:
- Revise and edit a draft of an informational text.
- Use nouns with matching verbs in statements about a story.

Additional Materials

Presentation BLMs 9 and 10
- Editing Checklist
- Singular and Plural Nouns with Matching Verbs Chart

Write Informational Text: Revise and Edit (10 MIN.) W.1.2, W.1.5, L.1.1c

Engage Thinking

Display the model draft from Day 3.

Say: *This is the first draft of my informational writing. Now we will revise and edit our drafts to make them stronger.*

Revise and Edit (iELD)

Model

Display your revised draft. Tell students that revising writing means to add or take away writing that makes the writing clearer, stronger, or more interesting. Editing is when a writer corrects errors that may make their writing hard to read. Use a think-aloud to model how you revised and edited the informational text.

> **Sample Modeled Writing**
>
> The butterfly is an insect with a unique life cycle. **The first stage of a butterfly's life is the egg stage. The egg is laid on a plant,** and a caterpillar grows inside the egg. **The** ~~bug~~ **caterpillar hatches and starts eating the plant leaves. It eats a lot and grows very quickly.** Soon it has a long, fat body. **The** ~~bug~~ **caterpillar changes to a pupa. The pupa can hang from a branch. The butterfly inside grows quickly. The butterfly comes out of the cocoon. It doesn't grow anymore, but it has large wings for flying.**

Sample think-aloud: *I wrote a draft about how butterflies change and grow. I revised and edited my draft to make it stronger and more interesting to read. First, I made my opening stronger. Then I added more detailed facts to help the reader understand the butterfly's life cycle. Finally, I made sure that I used the correct words to describe each stage of the life cycle.* **Bug** *is not an exact word. I made the writing better by replacing* **bug** *with the real scientific term,* **caterpillar***.*

Next, I corrected errors in spelling, grammar, and punctuation. I follow an editing checklist.

Editing	Check
I used pronouns correctly.	✓
I used correct end punctuation for each sentence.	✓
I used singular and plural nouns with matching verbs.	✓
I spelled all words correctly.	✓
I capitalized the first letter of the first word in each sentence.	✓

Editing Checklist

Practice

Invite partners to share the changes each of them plans to make to their essays. Each partner should share at least two changes he or she intends to make.

Independent Writing

Say: *Now it's your turn to write. Revise and edit your own draft to make it stronger.*

Students may write during writer's workshop time or at a writing station during small-group reading time. Independent Writing should occur before the Partner Share. Use the Build Language Review as needed while you confer and monitor.

Confer and Monitor

As students revise and edit independently, support their efforts as needed using prompts like those provided here.

Directive Feedback: *In your informational text, you want to use the correct words for each stage of the life cycle. Look back at the texts we have read, and look for the correct words.*

Self-Monitoring and Reflection: *What are some ways you could improve your word choice when you go back and revise?*

Validating and Confirming: *You used the term ___ to talk about ___. That word choice made you sound like an expert in your informational text!*

Partner Share

Say: *Now let's share our writing with our partners. Read your writing aloud. Point out the revisions and edits you made to improve your writing.*

Monitor partners as they share their writing.

Build Language Review: Singular and Plural Nouns and Matching Verbs

Review with students how to match singular and plural nouns with the correct verbs.

Say: *We have been learning about how singular and plural nouns and verbs match. You can match the correct verb with each singular or plural noun.*

Lead students in adding the correct verb to each sentence.

Sentences Without a Verb	Sentences With a Verb
Mother duck (lead/leads) her ducklings.	
The ducklings (tease/teases) the ugly duckling.	
The swans (is/are) nice to the ugly duckling.	

Oral Language Practice

Have partners write their own sentences using first singular and plural nouns and verbs correctly. For example: *The dogs run and play. The girl skips. The teacher reads.*

iELD Integrated ELD

Light Support
Make a list of the steps in the writing process. Have students name the steps and describe what happens in each step.

> **Writing Process**
> **Revise**—read again and improve (make better)
> **Edit**—correct errors (grammar, punctuation, spelling)
> **Publish**—prepare final (word process, online, print, or audio)

Moderate Support
As above, make a list of the steps in the writing process.
Ask: *What do we do when we revise? When we edit?* Work as a group to revise the sentence *There is an oak tree.*
Ask: *What can you add about the size of the tree? How has it changed?*

Substantial Support
Review the steps in the writing process as in the list above. Read the list aloud.
Help students revise a sentence by adding more detail.
Ask: *How can we add more detail to this sentence: There is an oak tree?*
Say: *Oak trees go through different stages in their life cycle. Oak trees can grow in many different places. After reading our sentence, the reader should know what life stage the oak tree is in, and where it is located. Let's work together to add these details to the sentence.*
Elicit: *There is a big oak tree in the yard.*

W.1.2 Write informative/explanatory texts in which they name a topic, supply some facts about the topic, and provide some sense of closure. **W.1.5** With guidance and support from adults, focus on a topic, respond to questions and suggestions from peers, and add details to strengthen writing as needed. **L.1.1c** Use singular and plural nouns with matching verbs in basic sentences (e.g., He hops; We hop).

The Ugly Duckling

Student Objectives

I will be able to:
• Share writing with a partner.
• Ask positive questions about a partner's writing.

Write Informational Text: Share

(10 MIN.) W.1.2, W.1.5

Engage Thinking

Explain to students that they have completed the brainstorming, planning, drafting, and revising and editing stages of their writing.

Say: *Now we are ready to share our final texts with the class. Part of sharing our writing is allowing our classmates to ask questions about our writing.*

Peer Collaboration Think-Aloud

Display the final version of the writing. Use a think-aloud to model how to ask questions about an informational text.

Sample Writing

The butterfly is an insect with a unique life cycle. The first stage of a butterfly's life is the egg stage. The egg is laid on a plant, and a caterpillar grows inside the egg. The caterpillar hatches and starts eating the plant leaves. It eats a lot and grows very quickly. Soon it has a long, fat body. The caterpillar changes to a pupa. The pupa can hang from a branch. The butterfly inside grows quickly. The butterfly comes out of the cocoon. It doesn't grow anymore, but it has large wings for flying.

Sample think-aloud: *I wrote about how butterflies change and grow. I completed the writing process, and now I'm ready to share my writing with the class. I know people will have questions about my writing. It is important to know how to ask questions, and what kinds of questions to ask.*

Modeled Peer Collaboration: Asking Questions

Think aloud as you model how to ask questions.

Sample think-aloud: *When I read someone else's writing and I want to ask questions, there are a few things to keep in mind: Be positive, kind, and write down your questions and answers.*

There are some questions that I think people may want to ask me about my writing. I will write these questions in a table. I can add the answers later.

Questions	Answers
Why did you decide to write about butterflies?	
What is the most interesting thing you learned about butterflies?	
What was the hardest thing about writing?	
What did you like the most about writing?	

Does anyone else have questions about my writing? We can add them to the table. Remember that the purpose of asking questions is to learn more about the topic, and to help the writer improve their writing the next time.

Practice Peer Collaboration

Say: *Now it's your turn to ask questions. Share your writing with a partner. Ask your partner questions about their writing. Remember to keep your questions positive and kind.*

Students may write during writer's workshop time or at a writing station during small-group reading time.

Whole-Group Share

Select a few volunteers to share their informational writing with the class.

Say: *Now let's share our writing with the class. After a student reads their writing aloud, we will all practice asking questions about the writing.*

Monitor students as they share their writing with the class and ask questions.

iELD Integrated ELD

Light Support
Give students an informational paragraph to read with a partner. Have partners make a list of questions to ask the author about their writing.

Moderate Support
Give student pairs an informational paragraph to read together. Provide sentence frames that can help students think of questions they can ask the writer. For example:
Why did you write about _____?
What else can you tell me about _____?
What is the most interesting thing about _____?
What was the most challenging thing to write about _____?

Substantial Support
Write original informational paragraphs on index cards and give each student pair one to read together. Explain to students that you are the author of these paragraphs. Give students a list of common questions to ask a writer. Have students choose two of the questions and ask you those questions.

W.1.2 With guidance and support from adults, focus on a topic, respond to questions and suggestions from peers, and add details to strengthen writing as needed. **W.1.5** With guidance and support from adults, focus on a topic, respond to questions and suggestions from peers, and add details to strengthen writing as needed.

The Fox and the Little Red Hen

Student Objectives

I will be able to:
- Brainstorm ideas to use to write in a narrative.
- Use commas in a series.

Additional Materials

Presentation BLMs 11 and 12
- Brainstorming Chart
- Commas Chart

Write a Narrative: Brainstorm (10 MIN.)

W.1.3, L.1.2c

Engage Thinking

Remind students that they have followed the steps in the writing process to write stories and nonfiction texts. Explain to students that they will be writing a folktale this week.

Say: *Remember that a folktale is a narrative that often uses animal characters to teach a lesson. The animal characters act and talk like people. Let's brainstorm ideas for our folktales.*

Brainstorm

Model

Remind students that the first step in the writing process is brainstorming. Explain that when a writer brainstorms, they think about what to write about. Tell students that folktales are stories, so they need to think of characters, a setting, and plot events to include in their story. Folktales also have a lesson, so students should think of a lesson to share with their readers.

Sample think-aloud: *Let's think of ideas for characters. Folktale characters are often talking animals. What animals should I write about? I'm going to write my ideas down. I could start with a spider. What other animals can I include. Flies and spiders go together. Spiders eat flies. Next, I will need to pick a setting. Where can the animals we've picked live? An attic would be a good place. Spiders spin webs and an attic is a good place for a web. Now I need a plot. I know spiders eat flies, so my story can be about a fly who trusts a spider. But the spider proves she is not a friend. The fly can learn the lesson that you should be careful who to trust.*

Characters	Setting	Events
Spider Fly	Attic	Fly asks spider for help. Spider tries to eat fly. Fly learns to be careful who she trusts.

Sample Brainstorming Chart

Practice (IELD)

Have students work with a partner to create brainstorming charts of their own. Students should take turns adding characters, setting details, and plot events to the chart.

Independent Writing

Say: *Now it's your turn to write. Brainstorm your own ideas for writing a folktale.*

Students may write during writer's workshop time or at a writing station during small-group reading time. Independent Writing should occur before the Partner Share. Use the Build Language Review as needed while you confer and monitor.

Confer and Monitor

As students brainstorm independently, support their efforts as needed using prompts like those provided here.

Directive Feedback: *Think about all the folktales we have read. Close your eyes and visualize the characters we have read about. Now write the names of those characters.*

Self-Monitoring and Reflection: *Think about the lessons we learned from the folktales we've read. A lesson is an important bit of advice you give to somebody. What lesson did you think was the best advice? What advice do you want to give readers?*

Validating and Confirming: *You brainstormed several ideas that you could develop!*

Partner Share

Invite students to share one of their ideas with a partner. Instruct them to follow the rules for collaborative conversation by listening to their partner and taking turns.

Build Language Review: Use Commas in a Series of Words

Remind students that when they list more than two words in a series, they must separate the words with commas.

Say: *Remember that a comma is a signal for you to pause when you read something. Where would you add commas in the following sentence?* Fox sat waited and pounced when Little Red Hen came home.

Lead students in adding commas to each sentence in the chart below.

Sentences Without Commas	Sentences With Commas
Fox was crafty sly and tricky.	
Little Red Hen was smart patient and brave.	
Fox felt hot tired and sweaty on the way home.	

Oral Language Practice
Have partners write and say their own sentences with commas related to the story. For example: *Mother Fox cooked, read, and cleaned in the story. Fox hid, pounced, and spun around in Little Red Hen's house.*

iELD Integrated ELD

Light Support
Have students work with a partner to think of topic ideas for their folktales. Have students make a list of their ideas and talk with their partner about which idea is best.

Moderate Support
Remind students that folktales usually teach a lesson.
Say: *A lesson is something that a character learns.* Have students work in small groups to list topics and lessons covered in folktales they have read or heard before.

Substantial Support
Have students work with a partner. Ask them to talk about lessons learned in folktales they have read or heard. Have students complete a sentence frame about the folktales.
When I read _____, I learned _____.

W.1.3 Write narratives in which they recount two or more appropriately sequenced events, include some details regarding what happened, use temporal words to signal event order, and provide some sense of closure. **L.1.2c** Use commas in dates and to separate single words in a series.

The Fox and the Little Red Hen

Student Objectives

I will be able to:
• Make a plan for writing a narrative.
• Use commas in dates and in a series.

Additional Materials

Presentation BLMs 13 and 14
• Planning Chart
• Commas Chart

Write a Narrative: Plan (10 MIN.) W.1.3, L1.2c

Engage Thinking

Tell students that now that they have selected a topic and characters, they are ready to plan their writing.

Plan

Model

Use a think-aloud to model how to plan the plot of a narrative.

Sample think-aloud: *We have brainstormed ideas for our own folktales. Now, we are going to write down the key events in our folktales. I am writing a folktale about a fly who trusts a spider. One event that will drive the plot is when the fly asks the spider for help. I will write that down as my first big idea! Next, I'll fill in the rest of the events I brainstormed.*

Big Ideas	Details
Fly asks spider for help.	
Spider tricks fly to come to her web.	
Spider tries to grab the fly.	
Fly escapes.	

Sample think-aloud: *Now, I need to write out the key details that are going to structure each event.*

Big Ideas	Details
Fly asks spider for help.	• Fly is trapped in an attic. • She flies until she gets tired. • She sees the spider's web and goes to ask for help.
Spider tricks fly to come to her web.	• The fly explains that she is lost. • The spider says the way out is through her web. • Fly flies toward the web.
Spider tries to grab the fly.	• Fly gets stuck on the web. • Spider tells Fly that she is going to be dinner. • Spider jumps to grab Fly.
Fly escapes.	• Fly pulls free of the web. • Fly flies away from spider. • Fly thinks that it is better to be alone than have bad friends.

Sample Planning Chart

Practice

Invite partners to add details to the Spider and Fly story plan. Partners should take turns thinking of details to add.

Independent Writing (IELD)

Say: *Now it's your turn to write. Write the big ideas and the key details you will include in your own folktale.*

Students may write during writer's workshop time or at a writing station during small-group reading time. Independent Writing should occur before the Partner Share. Use the Build Language Review as needed while you confer and monitor.

Confer and Monitor

As students plan independently, support their efforts as needed using prompts like those provided here.

Directive Feedback: *Visualize big ideas from your folktale. What details do you see in the picture in your mind?*

Self-Monitoring and Reflection: *Look at your big ideas and details. Do you have a clear beginning, middle, and end to your folktale? Why, or why not?*

Validating and Confirming: *Your details really help me visualize the characters and the big ideas in your folktale!*

Partner Share

Say: *Now let's share our plan with our partners. Read your writing aloud.*

Monitor partners as they share their writing.

Build Language Review: Use Commas in Dates and to Separate Words in a Series

Remind students that there are different uses for commas. Write today's date on the board. Have a volunteer add a comma in the correct place. Write a sentence with three or more items in a series on the board. Have a volunteer add commas in the correct places.

Say: *Who can show me how to use a comma in a date? Who can show me how to use commas in a series?*

Lead students in adding commas to each sentence and each date in the chart below.

Sentences/Dates Without Commas	Sentences/Dates With Commas
Little Red Hen is smart brave and clever.	[Little Red Hen is smart, brave, and clever.]
Mother Fox is patient caring and loving.	[Mother Fox is patient, caring, and loving.]
January 1 2018	[January 1, 2018]

Oral Language Practice

Have partners write and say their own sentences with either a date or a list with proper comma usage. For example: *I helped my parents by washing the plates, cups, and spoons. I like to play soccer, baseball, and basketball. My sister was born on May 4, 2011.*

iELD Integrated ELD

Light Support
Give students index cards that they can write the events in their folktales on. Guide students to talk about and then write one big idea on each card, then work with a partner to write supporting details for each big idea.

Moderate Support
Give students index cards that they can use to write the events in their folktales on. Write a sentence frame on each index card.
The first big idea is _____.
Guide students to use the sentence frame to talk about their ideas, and then discuss key details for that big idea with other sentence frames you supply.

Substantial Support
Give students index cards that they can refer to in order to talk about the events in their folktales. On each index card, write a sentence frame, such as *The first big idea is _____. One detail is _____.*
Students can complete each sentence frame.

W.1.3 Write narratives in which they recount two or more appropriately sequenced events, include some details regarding what happened, use temporal words to signal event order, and provide some sense of closure. **L.1.2c** Use commas in dates and to separate single words in a series.

The Fox and the Little Red Hen

Student Objectives

I will be able to:
- Write a draft of a narrative.
- Use adjectives in sentences.

Additional Materials

Presentation BLM 15
- Adjectives Chart

Write a Narrative: Draft (10 MIN.) W.1.3, L.1.1f

Engage Thinking

Tell students that now that they have completed their planning, it is time to write a draft of their narrative.

Say: *When you write a draft, you follow the plan you made for your narrative. All of your sentences should help develop the story or move the plot forward. You should include details that help the reader visualize and write an introduction and a conclusion.*

Draft

Model

Display and read aloud your draft. Then use a think-aloud to discuss what you did.

Sample Draft

One day, Fly was trapped in an attick. She flew around the attick looking for an exit. In a dark corner of the attick, she saw a spider sitting in a web. She did not trust spiders, but she was so tired. She flew over to Spider and asked, "Excuse me. I'm lost and I'm looking for an exit."

Spider smiled and said, "The exit is here. Just fly through my web"

"Thank you," said Fly.

Fly flew into Spider's web and got stuck! Spider laughed and said, "Now you are going to be my dinner!"

Fly broke free from the web and flew away as fast as she could!

Sample think-aloud: *I used my plan to write a draft of my folktale. My big ideas became the beginning, middle, and end of my story.*

Then I added some details about the setting and the characters. Spider lives in "a dark corner of the attic" and Fly feels "so tired."

Finally, I added some dialogue between Spider and Fly and used exclamation points to make sure the exciting parts—when Fly is caught and when she escapes—really stick out.

Practice

Invite partners to discuss the folktale they will write. Have them tell their partners what descriptive details they might use and what dialogue, if any, they might add. Partners should feel free to suggest strong details or help craft dialogue.

Independent Writing

Say: *Now it's your turn to write. Write a draft of your own folktale using the plan you created.*

Students may write during writer's workshop time or at a writing station during small-group reading time. Independent Writing should occur before the Partner Share. Use the Build Language Review as needed while you confer and monitor.

Confer and Monitor

As students draft independently, support their efforts as needed using prompts like those provided here.

Directive Feedback: *Look at your planning chart. What comes first in your folktale? How does the folktale build in the middle? How do you end your folktale?*

Self-Monitoring and Reflection: *Did you look at the details on your planning chart? How can you add more description to them to make them even stronger?*

Validating and Confirming: *You have made great progress today writing your stages and facts down!*

Partner Share

Say: *Now let's share our writing with our partners. Read your writing aloud. Point out how your draft follows the plan you created.*

Monitor partners as they share their writing.

Build Language Review: Use Adjectives (iELD)

Remind students that adjectives are words that describe people, places, and things.

Say: *Let's brainstorm a list of adjectives that describe each character in "The Fox and the Little Red Hen."*

Display the chart below and lead students in writing adjectives that describe each character.

Character	Adjectives
Little Red Hen	
Fox	
Mother Fox	

Oral Language Practice

Have partners write and say at least three adjectives to describe how they see themselves. For example: *beautiful, smart, fast, kind.*

Integrated ELD

Light Support
Review *The Fox and the Little Red Hen.* Have student pairs choose a character from the folktale and complete the chart below.

Character	Adjectives
Fox	embarrassed

Ask student pairs to practice using adjectives in sentences by generating a sentence that describes the character they chose. Provide sentence frames, if needed.
Fox felt _____.
Fox was _____.

Moderate Support
Prompt students to look for adjectives in *The Fox and the Little Red Hen* that describe Little Red Hen. Record students' responses in a chart.

Character	Adjectives
Little Red Hen	hardworking

Ask student pairs to practice using adjectives by completing sentence frames, such as:
Little Red Hen went out every morning to _____ for her food, I think it showed that she was a _____ hen.

Substantial Support
Prompt students to look for adjectives in *The Fox and the Little Red Hen* that describe Little Red Hen. Record students' responses in a chart.

Character	Adjectives
Little Red Hen	content

As a group, practice using adjectives in sentences. Write a description of Little Red Hen on the board and have volunteers come up to the board and underline the adjectives.
Sample description: *I think she was a content hen because she was rocking and smiling.*

W.1.3 Write narratives in which they recount two or more appropriately sequenced events, include some details regarding what happened, use temporal words to signal event order, and provide some sense of closure. **L.1.1f** Use frequently occurring adjectives.

Chicken Little & The Fox and the Little Red Hen

Student Objectives

I will be able to:
• Revise and edit a draft of a narrative.
• Use adjectives in sentences.

Additional Materials

Presentation BLMs 16 and 17
• Editing Checklist
• Adjectives Chart

Write a Narrative: Revise and Edit (10 MIN.) W.1.3, L.1.1f

Engage Thinking

Display the first draft you wrote yesterday. Explain that it is important to revise and edit a draft to make your writing the strongest it can be.

Say: *Now I am going to read my draft carefully and see where I can make my story stronger. I will also use the Editing Checklist to correct any mistakes in my writing.*

Revise and Edit (IELD)

Model

Use a think-aloud to revise and edit your draft.

Sample think-aloud: *Now that I have completed my draft, I will reread what I wrote and ask myself what I could do to make my writing even stronger.*

• *Does my story have a beginning, a middle, and an end? It does: Fly gets lost, Fly gets caught by Spider, and Fly escapes.*
• *Did I use enough adjectives in my descriptions so the reader can picture what I am describing? I think I should make my descriptions more detailed. Spider needs to be scarier. I will also describe Fly struggling to get out of the web.*
• *I should add a stronger ending. Folktales are supposed to have a lesson, so I'll have Fly tell readers the lesson.*
• *Finally, I use the Editing Checklist to check for spelling and punctuation errors. I see I spelled* **attic** *wrong! There's no* **k** *at the end. I make sure I spell it right every time I wrote it. I also see that one of my sentences doesn't have a period. I need to use punctuation to end my sentence correctly.*

Sample Revised and Edited Writing

One day, Fly was trapped in an attic. She flew around the attic looking for an exit. In a dark corner of the attic, she saw a large, hairy spider with sharp fangs sitting in a web. She did not trust spiders, but she was so tired. She flew over to Spider and asked, "Excuse me. I'm lost and I'm looking for an exit."

Spider smiled and said, "The exit is here. Just fly through my web."

"Thank you," said Fly.

Fly flew into Spider's web and got stuck! Spider laughed and said, "Now you are going to be my dinner!"

Fly kicked and screamed. She broke free from the web and flew away as fast as she could! As she flew away, Fly thought to be more careful about who she trusted.

Practice

Invite partners to read their writing out loud and look at their folktales together. Remind them to use the Editing Checklist as a guide for the types of errors to look for in their folktales. Encourage students to find at least one way to improve their partners' writing.

Independent Writing

Say: *Now it's your turn. Read your draft carefully. Find sentences or descriptions that you think could be stronger and revise them. Fix any mistakes you find.*

Students may write during writer's workshop time or at a writing station during small-group reading time. Independent Writing should occur before the Partner Share. Use the Build Language Review as needed while you confer and monitor.

 ## Confer and Monitor

As students revise and edit independently, support their efforts as needed using prompts like those provided here.

Directive Feedback: *Does your folktale have everything you need for a strong story: characters, a setting, and plot events? How about a lesson for the readers? Add anything you think might be missing?*

Self-Monitoring and Reflection: *Where are some places that you could change your word choice to improve your sentences when you go back and revise?*

Validating and Confirming: *I really like the way your folktale shows readers your lesson.*

Partner Share

Say: *Now let's share our writing with our partners. Read your writing aloud. Point out the revisions and edits you made to improve your writing.*

Monitor partners as they share their writing.

Build Language Review: Use Adjectives

Remind students that they have been learning about how to use adjectives in sentences. Have students reread their folktales and identify any adjectives they used.

Say: *Think about what an adjective is. It is a word that describes a person, place, or thing. We can use adjectives to make descriptions fuller and sentences more interesting.*

Lead students in writing adjectives to fill in the blanks in each sentence in the chart below.

Sentences	Adjectives
The _____ fox tries to trick Little Red Hen.	
Little Red Hen put a _____ in the bag.	
Little Red Hen lived in a _____ house near the woods.	

Oral Language Practice

Have partners write and say sentences with adjectives that describe Little Red Hen, Fox, and Mother Fox. For example: *Little Red Hen is smart and dizzy. Fox is crafty and mean. Mother Fox is sad and patient.*

W.1.3 Write narratives in which they recount two or more appropriately sequenced events, include some details regarding what happened, use temporal words to signal event order, and provide some sense of closure. **L.1.1f** Use frequently occurring adjectives.

---

iELD Integrated ELD

Light Support
Review the Model section and chart. Have students answer **who, what, when, where, how,** and **why** questions that help them focus on the revising task.

Moderate Support
Give students a sentence frame to help them answer the questions.
When I revise, I need to decide _____.

Substantial Support
Have students reread their drafts with a partner. Ask students to think about what decisions they need to make when they revise. *When I revise, I need to decide why a character should do something.* Give students a sentence frame to help them answer the questions.
When I revise, I need to decide _____.

Write a Narrative: Share (10 MIN.)

W.1.3, W.1.5, SL.1.1a

Mentor Read-Alouds, Vol. 1, pp. 28–29, Unit 4 Opener

Student Objectives

I will be able to:
- Share writing with a partner.
- Give a partner suggestions on how to improve their writing.

Engage Thinking

Explain to students that they have completed the brainstorming, planning, drafting, and revising and editing stages in the writing process.

Say: *Now we are ready to share our final folktale with the class. Part of sharing writing is giving suggestions to our classmates on how to make their writing even stronger.*

Peer Collaboration Think-Aloud

Display the final version of the folktale. Use a think-aloud to model how to give constructive suggestions to improve a narrative.

Sample Writing

One day, Fly was trapped in an attic. She flew around the attic looking for an exit. In a dark corner of the attic, she saw a large, hairy spider with sharp fangs sitting in a web. She did not trust spiders, but she was so tired. She flew over to Spider and asked, "Excuse me. I'm lost and I'm looking for an exit."

Spider smiled and said, "The exit is here. Just fly through my web."

"Thank you," said Fly.

Fly flew into Spider's web and got stuck! Spider laughed and said, "Now you are going to be my dinner!"

Fly kicked and screamed. She broke free from the web and flew away as fast as she could! As she flew away, Fly thought to be more careful about who she trusted.

Sample think-aloud: *I wrote a folktale about the importance of earning people's trust. I completed the writing process, and now I'm ready to share my writing with the class. I know that my classmates will have suggestions of how to improve my writing. I will give suggestions to my classmates as well. It is important to know how to give helpful suggestions in a nice way.*

Modeled Peer Collaboration (iELD)

Think aloud as you model how to give suggestions.

Sample think-aloud: *When I want to give a suggestion about somebody else's writing, there are some things I need to keep in mind. First, a good suggestion is kind and helpful. Second, a good suggestion is specific and improves the writing. Here are some suggestions for improving my folktale.*

Suggestions
Adding more descriptive words about the attic would help readers visualize the setting.
It would be interesting to know if Fly ever got out of the attic.
I could better picture Fly if you used more adjectives to tell what she looked like.

Suggestions Chart

Ask: *Does anybody else have suggestions for my writing? I can add them to this list. Remember that the reason we give suggestions is to help writers make good stories even better!*

Practice Peer Collaboration

Say: *Now it's your turn to give suggestions. Share your writing with a partner. Give your partner suggestions on how to improve their writing. Remember to keep your suggestions positive and kind.*

Students may write during writer's workshop time or at a writing station during small-group reading time.

Whole-Group Share

Select a few volunteers to share their folktales with the class.

Say: *Now let's share our writing with the class. After a student reads his or her writing aloud, we will all practice giving suggestions for making the writing even stronger.*

Monitor students as they share their writing with the class and give suggestions.

(iELD) Integrated ELD

Substantial Support
Give students a short folktale to read with a partner. Have partners make a list of suggestions they would give to the author to improve the story.

Moderate Support
Give students a short folktale to read with a partner. Provide each student pair with sentence frames that can help students think of suggestions they can give to the author.
You can make your writing more interesting by adding _____.

You can change _____ to make it easier to understand.

Light Support
Write original folktales on index cards and give each student pair one to read together. Explain to students that you are the author of these folktales. Give students a list of common suggestions writers can give each other on how to improve their writing. Have students choose the two suggestions that they think will best improve the folktale.

W.1.3 Write narratives in which they recount two or more appropriately sequenced events, include some details regarding what happened, use temporal words to signal event order, and provide some sense of closure. **W.1.5** With guidance and support from adults, focus on a topic, respond to questions and suggestions from peers, and add details to strengthen writing as needed. **SL.1.1a** Follow agreed-upon rules for discussions (e.g., listening to others with care, speaking one at a time about the topics and texts under discussion).

Technology Breakdown and *Using Technology at Work*

Student Objectives

I will be able to:
- Brainstorm ideas to write in an opinion text.
- Identify and use prepositions that tell *where* and *when*.

Additional Materials

Presentation BLM 18
- Brainstorming Chart

Write Opinion Text: State an Opinion

(10 MIN.) W.1.1, L.1.1i

Engage Thinking

Display *Using Technology at Work* and *Technology Breakdown*. Remind students that they have followed the steps of the writing process to write several different kinds of stories and texts. Explain that this week students will use the writing process to write an opinion text. First, they will brainstorm and plan their opinion. Then they will write a draft of their opinion. Finally, they will edit, revise, and share their opinion.

Say: *You will work on one piece of writing this week. You will follow the steps in the writing process. You are going to write an opinion telling readers which of the two books is better.*

Brainstorm

Model

Remind students that the first step in the writing process is brainstorming. When writers brainstorm, they think of ideas to write about. Model using a graphic organizer to help you brainstorm ideas. Think aloud as you write down details and impressions from each story.

Sample think-aloud: *First, I am going to write down details about technology from each story. I will also include my feelings about each story.*

Using Technology at Work	Technology Breakdown
I learned about many different jobs. I use technology when I work too.	I learned about one new job. I sometimes need help when my computer breaks down.
I learned how technology helps people. Technology helps me stay in touch with people.	The people in the story seem like they need help all the time. I need help sometimes, but not that often.
I read this story and was excited to learn about neat new technologies that other people use at work.	It was a funny story. I liked the funny illustrations and it was nice to hear the daughter discuss how much she likes watching her father help people.

Sample Brainstorming Chart

Sample think-aloud: *Let's look back at each book and write what we liked about each one on the chart. Now I'll look at the ideas in the chart to help me decide which book I liked best.* Using Technology at Work *had a lot of new facts about how different people use technology.* Technology Breakdown *was a funny story. However, I liked* Using Technology at Work *a little bit more than* Technology Breakdown*. I like using technology and learning about new technologies. My opinion is that I like* Using Technology at Work *the best.*

Practice

Now distribute blank Brainstorming Charts to the students. Ask students to brainstorm and decide which of the two books they think is better. Remind them that, because they are stating an opinion, their ideas can be different than someone else's. Ask them to share which text they prefer with a partner.

Independent Writing

Say: *Now it's your turn to brainstorm. Brainstorm your own ideas. Which book did you like best?*

Students may work during writer's workshop time or at a writing station during small-group reading time. Independent Writing should occur before the Partner Share and Build Language Review activities.

 Confer and Monitor

As students brainstorm independently, support their efforts as needed using prompts like those provided here.

Directive Feedback: *Think about the text and the story we read. Close your eyes and imagine the technology you've learned about and the way people use it. Now write down the ideas and images that come to your mind.*

Self-Monitoring and Reflection: *Think about what you enjoy in the things you read. Use what you like and dislike to help you decide what to write about.*

Validating and Confirming: *Good work! You brainstormed lots of great ideas.*

Partner Share

Invite students to share one of their ideas with a partner. Instruct them to follow the rules for collaborative conversation by listening to their partner and taking turns.

Build Language Review: Use Prepositions

Divide the students into two groups. Tell students that they are going to look for prepositions in *Technology Breakdown*.

- Group 1 will find prepositions that tell when something happens. When they find a preposition that tells when something happens, they should write the sentence in a list and underline the preposition.
- Group 2 will find prepositions that tell where something happens. When they find a preposition that tells where something happens, they should write the sentence in a list and underline the preposition.

After the groups are done, have them share their lists. Have the class check the groups' work together.

Oral Language Practice

Ask students to act out an action from *Technology Breakdown*. Call on volunteers to guess what action the student is acting out. All guesses must be in the form of a sentence with a preposition.

W.1.1 Write opinion pieces in which they introduce the topic or name the book they are writing about, state an opinion, supply a reason for the opinion, and provide some sense of closure. **L.1.1i** Use frequently occurring prepositions (e.g., during, beyond, toward).

(iELD) Integrated ELD

Elicit and discuss which story students liked better. Record their responses in a chart. Use the questions and specific support below to discuss and compare the stories.

Light Support

Using Technology at Work	Both	Technology Breakdown
Technology helps the workers.	show different kinds of technology	Technician helps the workers and fixes the technology.

Ask: *What did you like about each story? Did you like one story better than the other? Which one?*

Moderate Support

Using Technology at Work	Both	Technology Breakdown
has photos	describes real technology	has illustrations

I liked ___ better.

Substantial Support

Using Technology at Work	Both	Technology Breakdown
real people in many workplaces	show people using technology	one setting, the office

I liked ___ better.

Technology Breakdown

Student Objectives

I will be able to:
- Plan how to organize an opinion text.
- Use prepositions that tell where and when.

Additional Materials

Presentation BLMs 19 and 20
- Planning Chart
- Prepositions Chart

Write Opinion Text: Plan (10 MIN.) W.1.1, L.1.1i

Engage Thinking

Display and review the Brainstorming Chart created in the Day 1 writing lesson.

Say: *We spent time listing what we liked about* Using Technology at Work *and* Technology Breakdown. *Then we used those details to help us form an opinion about which book we liked best. Now we will plan our writing. We will decide how to state our opinion, what evidence to use, and what order we should put our evidence in.*

Plan

Model

Continue to display the Brainstorming Chart. Think aloud to demonstrate how to structure an opinion piece so that it includes a statement of the opinion, multiple pieces of evidence, and a close that restates the opinion.

Sample think-aloud: *After brainstorming, I decided that I would write about* Using Technology at Work. *Now I need to organize what I can write. I'll make a table that includes a statement of my opinion. I'll make room for two pieces of support. I also need to plan to close my opinion by restating what I think.*

Part of Writing	Details
Open: state opinion	
Support 1: learned about new careers	
Support 2: shows how technology really helps people	
Close: restate the opinion	

Sample Planning Chart

Sample think-aloud: *Now that I have an overall plan. I'll fill in the details for each section.*

Part of Writing	Details
Open: state opinion	*Using Technology at Work* is the better book.
Support 1: learned about new careers	• cartoonists—use computers to finish their art
Support 2: shows how technology really helps people	• firefighters—find people trapped in smoky buildings with a special camera
Close: restate the opinion	*Using Technology at Work* shows you how real people use technology to work better and save lives.

Sample Planning Chart

Practice

Invite students to add their own details to your plan. Ask partners to look at the Brainstorming Chart to identify reasons and details that support your opinion.

© Benchmark Education Company, LLC

Independent Writing

Distribute blank Planning Charts to your students.

Say: *Now it's your turn to create your own Planning Chart.*

Students may write during writer's workshop time or at a writing station during small-group reading time. Independent Writing should occur before the Partner Share. Use the Build Language Review as needed while you confer and monitor.

✔ Confer and Monitor

As students plan independently, support their efforts as needed using prompts like those provided here.

Directive Feedback: *Use the Brainstorming Charts you created to help you focus in on the details you should add to your plan.*

Self-Monitoring and Reflection: *Think about what you liked most about the book you chose. How can you communicate the things you enjoyed to your reader?*

Validating and Confirming: *Great plan! This will really help you when it comes time to draft your opinion.*

Partner Share

Say: *Now share your reason or reasons with a partner.*

Monitor partners as they share their plans. Remind them to take turns sharing and listening.

Build Language Review: Use Prepositions (iELD)

Remind students that they have learned how to use prepositions that tell when or where something happens. Invite students to suggest sentences using the prepositions **during, before, after, beyond, through,** and **into.** Ask volunteers to tell in which column of the chart each sentence should be written. For example:

When	Where
I drink water during dinner.	She runs through the grass.

Oral Language Practice

Have partners generate oral sentences to continue the chart above. Ask them to include one of the following prepositions in each of the sentences: **during, before, after, beyond, through, into.**

(iELD) Integrated ELD

Light Support
Use the two-column chart in Build Language Review. Have pairs place the preposition cards **next, over,** and **under** in the correct column of the chart.
Have students generate oral sentences using each preposition. Model forming a sentence for the preposition **next.**
Model: *I will visit Nome next year.*

Moderate Support
Use and review the two-column chart in Build Language Review. Write prepositions **since, in,** and **behind** on cards. Have partners take turns placing cards into the correct column of the chart.
Students should practice saying and then presenting sentences for each preposition. Model forming a sentence for the preposition **behind.**
Model: *The dog is behind the tree.*

Substantial Support
Use and review the two-column chart in Build Language Review. Write prepositions **until, on,** and **under** on cards. Have students echo-read. As you hold up each card, **ask:** *Does this preposition tell when or where?*
Have volunteers place the cards into the correct column of the chart. Model using a preposition in a sentence.
Model: *There was snow in Nome until March.*

W.1.1 Write opinion pieces in which they introduce the topic or name the book they are writing about, state an opinion, supply a reason for the opinion, and provide some sense of closure. **L.1.1i** Use frequently occurring prepositions (e.g., during, beyond, toward).

Technology Breakdown and *Using Technology at Work*

Student Objectives

I will be able to:
- Write a draft of an opinion text.
- Produce different kinds of sentences.

Write Opinion Text: Draft (10 MIN.) w.1.1, L.1.1j, L.1.2b

Engage Thinking

Remind students they have spent time deciding which book they like better: *Using Technology at Work* or *Technology Breakdown*.

Say: *We spent time listing what we liked about the selections we've read. Then we used that information to decide which book we liked best. After that, we determined the reasons for our opinion. Now we'll work together to write our opinion and reasons. This writing will be a draft.*

Draft

Model

Display and read aloud your draft. Note: the sample draft contains intentional errors that you will correct during the revision and editing step of the process. Then use a think-aloud to discuss what you did. Display your Planning Chart from Day 2 to consult.

Sample Modeled Writing

Using Technology at Work is the better book. Reading this book, I learned about new careers that use technology. Cartonists use computers to finish their art and mechanics use them too. This book also showed me how technology helps people in real life. Firefighters can use a special camera to find people trapped in smoky buildings. Pilots use technology to stop airplane accidents. *Using Technology at Work* shows how real people use technology to work better and save lives.

Sample think-aloud: *I used my plan to draft my opinion. First, I stated my opinion. That became my first sentence.*

Next, I followed my plan and added the reasons and supporting details I outlined. In my plan, these were just notes. I had to turn them into complete sentences.

Finally, I restated my opinion. I tell readers why I like Using Technology at Work, *but I say it in a new way. That is a strong way to finish an opinion piece.*

Practice

Have partners review the writing plans they created on Day 2. Do they have all the important elements of a strong opinion piece?

Independent Writing

Say: *Now it's your turn to write your opinion and reasons. Remember that this is a draft, which means you still have time to make your writing even better.*

Students may write during writer's workshop time or at a writing station during small-group reading time. Independent Writing should occur before the Partner Share. Use the Build Language Review as needed while you confer and monitor.

 **Confer and Monitor**

As students write independently, support their efforts as needed using prompts like those provided here.

Directive Feedback: *Look at your Planning Chart. What is the first thing you want to say in your opinion piece?*

Self-Monitoring and Reflection: *Look at your Planning Chart. Are you sticking to your plan or do you think you might need to change the plan a little to get your draft right?*

Validating and Confirming: *You have made great progress today writing a draft of your opinion and reasons!*

Partner Share

Say: *Now let's share our draft with our partners. Remember our classroom rules as you share your opinion and reasons.*

Monitor partners as they share their writing.

Build Language Review: Use Different Kinds of Sentences

Remind students that they have learned how to write different kinds of sentences.

Ask: *What can different kinds of sentences do or tell?*

Elicit that some sentences tell about things, some sentences ask questions, and other sentences express strong feelings. Ask students to suggest one example of each type of sentence. Remind them to tell which kind of punctuation goes with each type of sentence: period, question mark, or exclamation mark.

Oral Language Practice
Invite partners to create captions for the illustrations on pages 6–7 in *Technology Breakdown*. Remind them to use as many different types of sentences as they can.

 **Integrated ELD**

Light Support
Have partners work together. The first student tells which book he or she liked best. Then the second student asks, "Why?" The first student then replies using **because** to connect his or her opinion and reason. Have partners then switch roles and repeat. Remind students to reply in complete sentences.

Moderate Support
Have partners work together. The first student names his or her favorite book and points to a picture or illustration showing a detail he or she likes in that book. The second student asks, "Why?" The first student then replies using the sentence frame *I like ___ because ___.* Ask partners to switch roles and repeat.

Substantial Support
Display the books *Using Technology at Work* and *Technology Breakdown*. Ask a student to point to the book he or she likes best. Encourage him or her to complete the sentence *I like ___.* Ask the student "Why?" Have the student point to a picture or illustration he or she likes in one of the books. Help the student complete the phrase *because ___.*

W.1.1 Write opinion pieces in which they introduce the topic or name the book they are writing about, state an opinion, supply a reason for the opinion, and provide some sense of closure. **L.1.1j** Produce and expand complete simple and compound declarative, interrogative, imperative, and exclamatory sentences in response to prompts. **L.1.2b** Use end punctuation for sentences.

Write Opinion Text: Revise and Edit

(10 MIN.) W.1.1, W.1.5, L.1.1j, L.1.2b

Technology Breakdown and *Using Technology at Work*

Engage Thinking

Display the model draft from Day 3.

Say: *We all spent time writing our drafts to state our opinion and give reasons for our opinion. Now we'll revise and edit our writing. When we revise, we look at our sentences and see how we can make them even stronger. When we edit, we make corrections to fix any mistakes.*

Begin a brief revision/editing checklist. Invite students to make suggestions. See the checklist provided in the Model section for an example.

Student Objectives

I will be able to:
- Revise and edit a draft of an opinion text.
- Produce different kinds of sentences.

Additional Materials

Presentation BLM 21
- Editing Checklist

Revise and Edit

Model

Display your revised draft. Use a think-aloud to model how you revised and edited the opinion text.

Sample Modeled Writing

Using Technology at Work is the better book. Reading this book, I learned about new careers that use technology. Cartoonists use computers to finish their art and mechanics use computers to help them find out what is wrong with the machines they fix. This book also showed me how technology helps people in real life. Firefighters can use a special camera to find people trapped in smoky buildings. Pilots use technology to talk to other pilots in the air and avoid airplane accidents. *Using Technology at Work* shows how real people use technology to work better and save lives!

Sample think-aloud: *I say that mechanics use computers, but I don't say how. I'll add that to my support. I should also be specific about the technology that pilots use. Now, I will read the close of my opinion text. I want to add an exclamation mark at the end to show strong feeling. Next, I check my grammar and spelling. Oops, I see a mistake.* **Cartoonists** *is spelled with two* **o***'s. Now I've edited my writing. I'll reread my writing one more time. This is much stronger. Revising and editing really helped me improve my writing.*

Editing	Check
I used correct end punctuation for each type of sentence.	✓
I used prepositions correctly.	✓
I spelled all words correctly.	✓
I capitalized the first letter of the first word in each sentence.	✓

Editing Checklist

Practice

Ask partners to share the revisions or edits they each plan to make to their essays. Each partner should share at least two changes they intend to make.

Independent Writing

Say: *Now it's your turn to revise and edit your draft. Make your draft the best it can be.*

Students may revise and edit during writer's workshop time or at a writing station during small-group reading time. Independent Writing should occur before the Partner Share. Use the Build Language Review as needed while you confer and monitor.

☑ Confer and Monitor

As students revise and edit independently, support their efforts as needed using prompts like those provided here.

Directive Feedback: *You want to make sure you use the right terms for the job and technology you are writing about. Look back at the original text to find the correct words.*

Self-Monitoring and Reflection: *What are some ways you could add expression and power to your opinion? Think about word choice and using expressive punctuation.*

Validating and Confirming: *This is a clear opinion with strong support. Your use of _____ as an example really helps me understand why you like _____ best.*

Partner Share

Say: *Now let's share our writing with our partners. Point out the revisions and edits you made to improve your writing.*

Monitor partners as they share their thinking and writing.

Build Language Review: Use Different Kinds of Sentences

Remind students that they have learned about different types of sentences and the end punctuation mark that is appropriate for each kind.

Ask:
- *What sentence can you write that will use a period at the end?*
- *What sentence can you write that will use a question mark at the end?*
- *What punctuation mark do you put at the end of a sentence that shows strong feeling?*

Oral Language Practice
Have partners take turns asking each other questions about the illustrations in *Technology Breakdown.* After one partner asks a question, the other should respond using different kinds of sentences. For example, *How does the girl feel about the noise in the office? It's making her feel crazy! How does her dad feel when things go wrong? He feels calm.*

iELD Integrated ELD

Light Support
List, discuss, and then have students echo-read the steps in the revision/editing process. Help students focus on the writing task. Point to a sentence in your sample opinion text.
Ask: *How might I change this sentence?*

Moderate Support
List, discuss, and have students echo-read the steps in the revision/editing process.
Ask: *Why do we revise? How do we revise?*
Ask: *What punctuation might I need to change?*
Model rereading and fixing punctuation in one sentence from your sample opinion text.

Substantial Support
List, discuss, and have students echo-read the steps in the revision/editing process.
Write the following sentence on the board: *I love my computer.*
Model changing the period to an exclamation mark to show emotion: *I love my computer!*

W.1.1 Write opinion pieces in which they introduce the topic or name the book they are writing about, state an opinion, supply a reason for the opinion, and provide some sense of closure. **W.1.5** With guidance and support from adults, focus on a topic, respond to questions and suggestions from peers, and add details to strengthen writing as needed. **L.1.1j** Produce and expand complete simple and compound declarative, interrogative, imperative, and exclamatory sentences in response to prompts. **L.1.2b** Use end punctuation for sentences.

Technology Breakdown and *Using Technology at Work*

Student Objectives

I will be able to:
- Share writing with a partner.
- Compliment a peer's writing.
- Ask questions and make suggestions about a peer's writing.

Write Opinion Text: Share (10 MIN.) W.1.1, SL.1.1b, SL.1.1c

Engage Thinking

Explain to students that they have completed the brainstorming, planning, drafting, and revising and editing stages of their writing.

Say: *Now we are ready to share our final texts with the class. When sharing our writing, we have learned how to give compliments, ask questions, and offer suggestions. We are all going to practice these skills again today.*

Peer Collaboration Think-Aloud

Display the final version of the opinion text. Read your sample writing aloud.

Sample Writing

Using Technology at Work is the better book. Reading this book, I learned about new careers that use technology. Cartoonists use computers to finish their art and mechanics use computers to help them find out what is wrong with the machines they fix. This book also showed me how technology helps people in real life. Firefighters can use a special camera to find people trapped in smoky buildings. Pilots use technology to talk with other pilots in the air and avoid airplane accidents. *Using Technology at Work* shows how real people use technology to work better and save lives!

Sample think-aloud: *I wrote that I thought* Using Technology at Work *was the better book. I went through all the writing process steps. Now I'm ready to share my opinion writing and get feedback: compliments, questions, and suggestions.*

Model Peer Collaboration

Model the three feedbacks strategies the class has practiced: compliment, question, suggestion.

Compliment–Say: *Remember, compliments should be kind and specific. Find something that the writer did really well and compliment him or her on that. Looking at my opinion text, you might say, "I really liked your writing. You used four strong examples to support your opinion and that really helps me understand what you mean."*

Question–Say: *When I ask a writer a question about his or her work, I should ask it in a polite way and focus on an important idea in the writing. Looking at my writing, you could say, "I like all the examples you used. Why did you put them in the order you did? Why did you talk about new careers and then helpful technology?"*

Suggestion–Say: *When I offer a suggestion to a writer, I want to make sure that I'm polite, that my suggestion is specific, and that it will help the writer the next time he or she writes an opinion piece. Looking at my writing, you might say, "You do a great job of explaining why you like* Using Technology at Work. *Next time, you should add something about* Technology Breakdown *that explains why you did not pick it."*

Practice Peer Collaboration (iELD)

Say: *Now it's your turn to share your writing with a partner and practice one of the sharing skills we've learned. You chose what skill you will practice. Share your writing with a partner. Listen as your partner gives you a compliment, asks a question, or offers a suggestion. Remember to answer your partner if he or she asks you a question. Then switch roles.*

Students may collaborate during writer's workshop time or at a writing station during small-group reading time.

Whole-Group Share

Select a few volunteers to share their opinion text with the class.

Say: *Now let's share our writing with the class. After a student reads his or her writing aloud, we will all practice one of the three feedback strategies we've learned: giving compliments, asking questions, and making suggestions.*

Monitor students as they share their writing with the class and practice feedback strategies.

(iELD) Integrated ELD

Light Support
Review what a suggestion is. Ask student pairs to read and then make a suggestion about another student's writing. If needed, model an example exchange between you and a volunteer.

Moderate Support
Review what a suggestion is. Place students in pairs. Have each student practice making a suggestion for the other student's writing. Write these sentence frames on the board:
You could add _____ here.
One more ____ would ____.
Tell students to refer to the sentence frames if they have trouble phrasing their suggestion.

Substantial Support
Review what a suggestion is. Model an example exchange between you and a volunteer. Have the student read his or her final opinion piece and then give him or her a specific, focused suggestion. Then read your sample opinion piece and have students offer positive, productive suggestions.

W.1.1 Write opinion pieces in which they introduce the topic or name the book they are writing about, state an opinion, supply a reason for the opinion, and provide some sense of closure. **SL.1.1b** Build on others' talk in conversations by responding to the comments of others through multiple exchanges. **SL.1.1c** Ask questions to clear up any confusion about the topics and texts under discussion.

Read a Personal Narrative Mentor Text (10 MIN.) W.1.3

Engage Thinking

Explain that for the next two weeks, you will work together to write personal narratives.

Say: *A personal narrative tells a true story from the writer's life. When you write a personal narrative, you include details about where you were, what happened, and what you said and did. You also describe how you felt.*

Read the Mentor Text

Display and read aloud the following mentor text. When you finish, allow students to respond with comments or questions.

> **The Day I Slept Late**
> **by** _____
> I was excited to go fishing with my grandpa at Blue Lake. First, Grandpa helped me set the clock for 6:00. Then I went to sleep. I woke up at 8:00. The alarm did not go off! I was so surprised. Finally, I checked the clock, and we had set the alarm for 6:00 at night! I learned that we should pay close attention when setting an alarm for something important.

Mentor Personal Narrative

Analyze the Mentor Text

Say: *Let's use this text to analyze the parts, or features, of a personal narrative.*

As you go through the text, point out the following features and list them on a chart:

> A personal narrative has:
> • a title and author
> • a setting
> • people
> • events in the order they happened
> • the writer's reaction to the experience

Personal Narrative Anchor Chart

 Quick Write and Share

Say: *Today we will do something called a quick write. You will have five minutes to draw or write about something you did today. You can use the anchor chart to help you.*

Explain that this activity is a warm-up for writing a longer personal narrative later this week. When students finish, ask them to share their work with a partner.

Student Objectives

I will be able to:
• Identify the features of a personal narrative.
• Read and analyze a mentor text.
• Combine two simple sentences with a conjunction.

Additional Materials

• Writing portfolios
Presentation BLM 22
• Conjunctions Chart

Present Portfolios

Hand out prepared portfolios. These can be as simple as manila file folders labeled "Personal Narrative."

Say: *Here is a portfolio you may use to store all the writing you do for the next two weeks. This will help you organize your work and ideas so you can look back at them whenever you like.*

Allow time for students to write their names on their portfolios, file their quick-writes, and store the portfolios in a designated spot in the classroom.

Partner Share

Say: *Now let's share our writing with partners. First, name the kind of writing we've been talking about. Then read your sentence out loud.*

Monitor partners as they share their writing. Have students use the Anchor Chart to focus their discussion. Students should discuss what they've learned about each aspect of narratives indicated in the chart.

Build Language: Use Conjunctions

(10 MIN.) L.1.1g, L.1.1j

Display the words **and, but, or, so,** and **because**. Explain that these words are called conjunctions and are used to join two parts of a sentence.

Say: *Conjunctions can help a sentence flow more smoothly and explain the connections between ideas in a sentence. Add a comma before a conjunction when you form a compound sentence. Conjunctions **or** and **but** are used to show a difference. Conjunctions **because** and **so** can help tell why something happened.*

Display the following sentences and model using conjunctions to join them. Then have volunteers identify the conjunction in each new sentence.

Turtle is lazy. Turtle is selfish.	Turtle is lazy and selfish.
The geese warn Turtle. He keeps talking.	The geese warn Turtle, but he keeps talking.
Turtle can eat the apple. Turtle can eat the pear.	Turtle can eat the apple or the pear.
Turtle's shell cracks. He falls on some rocks.	Turtle's shell cracks because he falls on some rocks.

Oral Language Practice

Have partners ask each other the following questions and respond with a sentence that contains a conjunction: *What two words describe Turtle at the beginning of the story? Why do the animals grow tired of Turtle's laziness? What happens when the geese fly with Turtle? What lesson does Turtle learn?*

iELD Integrated ELD

Light Support
Display *Why Turtle's Shell Is Cracked.*
Ask: *What important event helped you understand that Turtle does something wrong?*
Create a chart to help organize students' thoughts.

Important Event	Turtle won't be quiet when he flies with the geese.
Opinion	is wrong, makes a bad decision, falls, and cracks his shell

Moderate Support
Display *Why Turtle's Shell Is Cracked.*
Ask: *What important event helped you understand that Turtle does something wrong?*
Have partners complete the sentence frame orally and in writing.
In my opinion, Turtle is __, __, and __ because __.
Record responses in a chart, such as:

Important Event	Turtle demands more food.
Opinion	is wrong, selfish, greedy

Substantial Support
Display and review *Why Turtle's Shell Is Cracked.*
Ask: *What important event helped you understand that Turtle does something wrong?*
Have partners complete the sentence frame orally and in writing.
I think Turtle is __, __, and __ because he __.
Record responses in a chart.

Important Event	Turtle makes animals bring him food.
Opinion	is wrong and lazy and thinks only about himself

W.1.3 Write narratives in which they recount two or more appropriately sequenced events, include some details regarding what happened, use temporal words to signal event order, and provide some sense of closure. **L.1.1g** Use frequently occurring conjunctions (e.g., and, but, or, so, because). **L.1.1j** Produce and expand complete simple and compound declarative, interrogative, imperative, and exclamatory sentences in response to prompts.

Personal Narrative: Brainstorm (10 MIN.)

W.1.3, L.1.1g, L.1.1j

Engage Thinking

Display the Mentor Text. Point to the title.

Say: *The title, or topic of the story, is what the author wrote about. This week you will write about a mistake you learned from. Today, I will think about ideas for a writing topic.*

Model

Use a think-aloud to model how to brainstorm ideas for a story topic.

Sample think-aloud: *I can think of mistakes I've made and what I learned from those mistakes. Let's brainstorm, or make a list of our ideas. After we have a list of ideas, we can choose one idea that is the best to write about.*

Create a topic list. For example:

> **Topic Ideas**
> 1. I went to a picnic on the wrong day.
> 2. I did not check the weather before leaving for school.
> 3. I slept late when I set the alarm for the wrong time.

Say: *Now I'll choose the topic I want to write about. I think I'd like to write about the time when I slept late. I'll put a star beside this topic.*

Practice

Say: *Turn and talk to your partner about a memory you would like to write about. Think about a time when you made a mistake and learned from it.*

✓ Quick Write

Say: *Now you will do another quick write. You will have five minutes to draw or write a list of topics you could use for a personal narrative. When you finish, put a star beside the topic you most want to write about. Then put your completed list in your personal narrative portfolio.*

Student Objectives

I will be able to:
• Brainstorm a list of topics to write about.
• Use conjunctions in compound sentences.

Additional Materials

• Writing portfolios
Presentation BLM 23
• Conjunctions Chart

Build Language Review: Use Conjunctions

Display the words **and, but, or, so,** and **because**. Remind students that these conjunctions are words that join two parts of a sentence.

Say: *Conjunctions **or** and **but** are used to show a difference. Conjunctions **because** and **so** can help tell why something happened.*

Display the following sentences and have students identify which conjunction competes each sentence.

The animals held a meeting ____ they could talk about Turtle.
Turtle could have been quiet, ____ he kept talking.
Turtle promised not to be greedy, ____ he got his own food.
Turtle's shell cracked ____ he landed on some rocks.
Do you think Turtle will be lazy ____ selfish anymore?

Oral Language Practice

Have partners work together to come up with two other ideas about how to deal with Turtle's laziness. Have them share their ideas with another pair using the conjunction **or**. Then have the four choose one of the ideas and explain why it works using the conjunction **because**. Encourage them to discuss what happens after the new plan is tried using the conjunctions **and, but**, or **so**.

---

iELD **Integrated ELD**

Light Support
Have students draw and label two pictures that show times they made a mistake and learned from it. Help students use their picture labels to write complete sentences that could be story topics. Have them read their sentences aloud and choose one to be their writing topic.

Moderate Support
Have students draw a picture of a time they made a mistake. Have them complete a sentence that tells their story topic.
I made a mistake when I ____. I learned ____.
Have students echo-read their sentences.

Substantial Support
Have students draw a picture of a time they made a mistake. Help them write a caption for the picture. Have them use the caption to write a sentence that tells their story topic.
I remember when I ____.
Have students echo-read their sentences.

W.1.3 Write narratives in which they recount two or more appropriately sequenced events, include some details regarding what happened, use temporal words to signal event order, and provide some sense of closure. **L.1.1g** Use frequently occurring conjunctions (e.g., and, but, or, so, because). **L.1.1j** Produce and expand complete simple and compound declarative, interrogative, imperative, and exclamatory sentences in response to prompts.

Personal Narrative: Planning (10 MIN.)

W.1.3, L.1.1g, L.1.1j

Engage Thinking

Review the Personal Narrative Anchor Chart you created on Day 1 and point out that one feature is "events in the order they happened." Then display the topic idea list you created on Day 2.

Say: *Yesterday, we each made a list of ideas for topics for our personal narratives. Then we put a star beside the topic we chose. Today we will plan our writing by listing the events of that topic in the order they happened.*

Topic Ideas
1. I went to a picnic on the wrong day.
2. I did not check the weather before leaving for school.
3. I slept late when I set the alarm for the wrong time.

Model

Pointing to the star on your list, remind students that you chose to write about a time when you slept late.

Sample think-aloud: *I remember events from the time I slept late. First, Grandpa helped me set the alarm for 6:00. Then I went to sleep and didn't wake up until 8:00! Finally, I checked the clock and realized I had set the alarm for the night.*

Beginning
Grandpa helped me set the clock for 6:00.
Middle
I went to sleep. I woke up at 8:00.
Ending
I checked the clock. We had set the alarm for 6:00 at night!

Practice

Invite partners to tell each other the events they want to include about their chosen topic, making sure to say them in the order they happened.

 Quick Write (IELD)

Say: *Now you will do another quick write. You will have five minutes write down your sequence of events. Make sure your events are in the proper order. You will use this sequence to help you write your personal narrative later. Put your completed sequence in your Personal Narrative portfolio.*

Student Objectives

I will be able to:
- List story events for my personal narrative.
- Identify conjunctions in compound sentences.

Additional Materials

- Writing portfolios

Presentation BLM 24
- Sequence of Events Chart

Build Language Review: Use Conjunctions

Display the words **and, but, or, so,** and **because**. Remind students that conjunctions are words that join two parts of a sentence.

Say: *The conjunction **and** joins two sentences, **or** and **but** show a difference, and **because** and **so** tell why something happened.*

Display the Mentor Text and ask students to identify any conjunctions and tell what they do. Then display the following sentences and ask to students identify each conjunction and tell what it does.

> Turtle demanded more food, but the animals had trouble finding it.
>
> The animals were tired of Turtle, so they made a plan.
>
> The geese picked up Turtle, and they carried him south.
>
> Turtle cried because his shell cracked.
>
> Turtle could choose to change or he could choose to stay selfish.

Oral Language Practice

Have partners look through *Why Turtle's Shell Is Cracked* to find conjunctions. When they identify a conjunction, have them take turns telling each other what the conjunction does.

Integrated ELD

Light Support
Lead students to draw three events in order in the boxes on the sequence chart. Ask them to talk about the sequence with a partner and then write a sentence for each picture. Help students with grammar and vocabulary as necessary.

Moderate Support
Label the three boxes on the sequence chart **1, 2,** and **3** to emphasize the order of events.
Have students draw three events in order in the boxes. Have students write a caption for each picture. Have students read their captions aloud.

Substantial Support
Label the three boxes on the sequence chart **1, 2,** and **3** and draw down arrows between each box to emphasize the order of events.
Have students draw three events in order in the boxes. Help students dictate a sentence for each picture. Have them echo-read each sentence. Supply sentence frames as needed to support their efforts, such as *First, the _____. Next, _____. At the end, _____.*

W.1.3 Write narratives in which they recount two or more appropriately sequenced events, include some details regarding what happened, use temporal words to signal event order, and provide some sense of closure. **L.1.1g** Use frequently occurring conjunctions (e.g., and, but, or, so, because). **L.1.1j** Produce and expand complete simple and compound declarative, interrogative, imperative, and exclamatory sentences in response to prompts.

Personal Narrative: Writing a Draft

(10 MIN.) W.1.3, L.1.1g, L.1.1j

Engage Thinking

Review the characteristics of a personal narrative on the Anchor Chart. Display and read the Model Sequence Chart from Day 2 with students.

Say: *Today we will use our sequence charts to write a draft of our personal narratives.*

Model

Work with students to write a personal narrative draft. Point out that they have chosen a topic and listed the events in order. As you write each sentence, model how you apply your knowledge of print concepts, phonics, high-frequency words, and English language conventions.

Sample Draft

I was excited to go fishing with my grandpa. Grandpa helped me set the clock for 6:00. I went to sleep. I woke up at 8:00. The alarm did not go off! I checked the clock. We had set the alarm for 6:00 at night!

Practice

Say: *Now turn to a partner and talk about the descriptive details and words you will add to your writing.*

Independent Writing (iELD)

Say: *Now it's your turn to write. Use the events from your sequence chart to write a first try of your story. Add any information that helps the reader understand what mistake you made and what you learned from it.*

Students may write during writer's workshop time or at a writing station during small-group reading time. Independent Writing should occur before the Partner Share. Use the Build Language Review as needed while you confer and monitor.

Student Objectives

I will be able to:
- Write a draft of a personal narrative.
- Write story events in order.
- Complete compound sentences.

Additional Materials

- Writing portfolios
Presentation BLM 25
- Conjunctions Chart

 **Confer and Monitor**

As students write independently, support their efforts as needed using prompts like those provided here.

Directive Feedback: *Look at your event planning chart to help you organize your ideas.*

Self-Monitoring and Reflection: *Show me where you can add more details.*

Validating and Confirming: *I really like how creative you were with your word choice.*

Partner Share

Say: *Now let's share our drafts with the group. Remember our three feedback skills: giving compliments, asking questions, and making suggestions. Pick one of those skills to practice now.*

Select a student as your partner and tell the class that you are going to practice giving a suggestion. Have your partner read their draft aloud. Then provide a suggestion that is positive, specific, and focused on improving your partner's draft. Then switch roles and model giving suggestions again.

Monitor partners as they share their drafts and provide feedback. Tell students to put their drafts in their personal narrative portfolios.

Build Language Review: Use Conjunctions

Remind students that they have been using conjunctions **and, but, or, so,** and **because** to join two parts of a sentence.

Display the following sentences. Ask students think about what each conjunction means and suggest an ending for the sentence.

> The animals are upset with Turtle because ___.
>
> Turtle goes with the geese, so ___.
>
> Turtle cries because ___.
>
> In the story, Turtle acts badly, but ___.

Oral Language Practice

Have partners work together to come up with their own endings to each sentence in the Build Language Review activity. Have them share their new sentences with another pair of students.

 **Integrated ELD**

Light Support

Display the Mentor Text. Have pairs identify the pronoun the author uses to show who is telling the story.

Help them conclude that **I** is used in place of the author's name when telling a personal narrative. Display the following sentences.

I woke up at 8:00. I checked the clock.

Have students circle the verb, or action word, in each sentence.

Have students write sentences from their sequence charts using **I** followed by an action word. Have students read their sentences aloud.

Moderate Support

Display the following sentences.

I woke up at 8:00. I checked the clock.

Point out that **I** is used in place of the author's name when telling a personal narrative.

Have students circle the verb, or action word, in the sentences. Point out that the verb follows **I**.

Have students write sentences from their sequence charts using **I** followed by an action word. Have pairs read each other's sentences aloud.

Substantial Support

Use the Mentor Text to model the use of **I**. Explain that they use **I** in place of their name when telling the story.

I woke up at 8:00. I checked the clock.

Point out that the verb, or action word, follows **I**.

Help students complete sentence frames that describe pictures in their sequence charts. Have students echo-read their sentences.

I ___.

W.1.3 Write narratives in which they recount two or more appropriately sequenced events, include some details regarding what happened, use temporal words to signal event order, and provide some sense of closure. **L.1.1g** Use frequently occurring conjunctions (e.g., and, but, or, so, because). **L.1.1j** Produce and expand complete simple and compound declarative, interrogative, imperative, and exclamatory sentences in response to prompts.

Personal Narrative: Add a Conclusion

(10 MIN.) W.1.3, L.1.1g, L.1.1j

Engage Thinking

Review the characteristics of a personal narrative on the Anchor Chart. Point out the final element on the Anchor Chart: the writer's reaction to the experience. Tell students that the end of their narrative will focus on what they learned from the events in their narrative. Tell them that they will also add a title to their narrative.

Model

Work with students to develop their drafts. Model adding a title and strong ending that captures the lesson learned to your sample writing. As you write each sentence, model how you apply your knowledge of print concepts, phonics, high-frequency words, and English language conventions.

> The Day I Slept Late
> I was excited to go fishing with grandpa. Grandpa helped me set the clock for 6:00. I went to sleep. I woke up at 8:00. The alarm did not go off! I checked the clock. We had set the alarm for 6:00 at night! I learned that we should pay close attention when setting an alarm for something important.

Sample Personal Narrative Draft

Practice (iELD)

Invite partners to read their draft out loud and look at it together. Have students to discuss titles and closing lessons with their partners. Suggest that students look back at their topics to write a title. To help them write a strong ending, tell them to focus on the lesson they would like a reader to learn.

Independent Writing

Say: *Now it's your turn work on your draft. Add a title that tells the topic of your personal narrative. Check to see if your story tells what you learned from your mistake. Add the lesson to make a strong ending.*

Students may write during writer's workshop time or at a writing station during small-group reading time. Independent Writing should occur before the Whole-Group Share. Use the Build Language Review as needed while you confer and monitor.

Student Objectives

I will be able to:
• Write a title for my personal narrative.
• Write a strong ending for my personal narrative.
• Use conjunctions in compound sentences.

Additional Materials

• Writing portfolios
Presentation BLM 26
• Conjunctions Chart

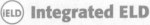

 **Confer and Monitor**

As students write independently, support their efforts as needed using prompts like those provided here.

Directive Feedback: *Use the following sentence frame to help you draft a close for your story:* I learned _____.

Self-Monitoring and Reflection: *Read your draft again. What detail strikes you as the most important? Turn that detail into your title.*

Validating and Confirming: *Good work! Your title really expresses what your story is about, and the lesson you share with the readers makes an excellent ending for your story.*

Whole-Group Share

Say: *Now let's share our writing with the group. First, read the title of your personal narrative. Then read your story out loud.*

Assist as needed as students share their writing with the group. Remind students to put their draft in their Personal Narrative Portfolio.

Build Language Review: Use Conjunctions

Tell students that they have been using conjunctions **and, but, or, so,** and **because** to join two parts of a sentence.

Display the following sentences. Ask students to suggest an ending for each sentence that includes a conjunction. Ask students to suggest endings that can be added to complete each compound sentence.

> The Great Turtle Leader is proud of his shell ____.
> Animals bring Turtle food _____.
> The animals grow tired of Turtle's ____.
> Things change when winter approaches, ____.

Oral Language Practice

Have pairs take turns telling each other what they liked and didn't like about *Why Turtle's Shell Is Cracked*. Encourage them to use sentences that include conjunctions.

W.1.3 Write narratives in which they recount two or more appropriately sequenced events, include some details regarding what happened, use temporal words to signal event order, and provide some sense of closure. **L.1.1g** Use frequently occurring conjunctions (e.g., and, but, or, so, because). **L.1.1j** Produce and expand complete simple and compound declarative, interrogative, imperative, and exclamatory sentences in response to prompts.

Personal Narrative: Revise to Add Time Words (10 MIN.) W.1.3, W.1.5, L.1.1g, L.1.1j

Engage Thinking

Display and read the fourth item on the Personal Narrative Anchor Chart: events in the order they happened. Remind students that strong writers revisit and revise their work to make their writing the strongest it can be.

Say: *Now that we have written our drafts, we're going to revise our work to make sure readers can understand what events happen in the beginning, middle, and end of our narrative.*

Model

Work with students to revise your personal narrative draft. Show them how to incorporate time order signal words such as **first, then,** and **finally** to describe the order of events. As you write each sentence, model how you apply your knowledge of print concepts, phonics, high-frequency words, and English language conventions.

The Day I Slept Late

I was excited to go fishing with my grandpa. First, grandpa helped me set the clock for 6:00. Then I went to sleep. I woke up at 8:00. The alarm did not go off! Finally, I checked the clock. We had set the alarm for 6:00 at night! I learned that we should pay close attention when setting an alarm for something important.

Sample Personal Narrative Draft

Practice

Have students read their personal narrative draft to their partner. Working together, students should identify points in their narrative where they could add a sequence signal word to show the order in which events occur. Write time order words such as **first, next, later, then,** and **finally** on the board.

Independent Writing

Say: *Now it's your turn to revise. Read the draft of your personal narrative and look for places where you can add time order words.*

Students may write during writer's workshop time or at a writing station during small-group reading time. Independent Writing should occur before the Partner Share. Use the Build Language Review as needed while you confer and monitor.

Student Objectives 📋

I will be able to:
• Use words that show order of events.
• Use conjunctions in compound sentences.

Additional Materials

• Writing portfolios
Presentation BLM 27
• Conjunctions Chart

Confer and Monitor

As students revise independently, support their efforts as needed using prompts like those provided here.

Directive Feedback: *Number the events that happen in your story. Now think of words that tell the order you showed with numbers. What time order word fits with number 1?*

Self-Monitoring and Reflection: *When you tell somebody the story without writing it down, listen for the time order words you use when you're just talking. What words do you hear yourself use?*

Validating and Confirming: *Great use of sequence words! I can really see how one event relates to the next in your story.*

Partner Share

Say: *Now let's share our writing with the group. Read your personal narratives aloud. Point out where you've added words that show the order of events in your story.*

Monitor partners as they share their writing. Remind students to put their revised draft in their Personal Narrative Portfolio.

Build Language Review: Use Conjunctions

Remind students that they have used conjunctions **and, but, or, so,** and **because**.

Say: *The conjunction **and** joins two sentences. The conjunctions **or** and **but** show a difference. The conjunctions **because** and **so** tell why something happened.*

Display the following sentences. Ask students which conjunction completes each sentence.

> Mosquito talks about huge yams, ___ Iguana does not believe him.
> Iguana doesn't want to hear Mosquito, ___ she puts sticks in her ears.
> Python hides in a hole ___ he thinks Iguana is angry with him.

Oral Language Practice

Have pairs read aloud the completed sentences from the Build Language Review activity and discuss what each conjunction does.

Integrated ELD

Light Support
Brainstorm time order words with students, grouping them under the headings **Beginning, Middle,** and **End.** Then have pairs take turns telling their personal narrative stories to each other. Finally, have them retell their stories using time order words.

Moderate Support
Have students write the time order words **first, next,** and **finally** on self-stick notes and match each word to the headings **Beginning, Middle,** or **End** on their Sequence Charts from last week.

Have partners tell the events on their sequence charts to each other using time order words **first, next,** and **finally**.

Substantial Support
Make a card with each time order word: **first, next, finally.** Have three students hold the cards and stand to show the correct order. Allow students to exchange cards and reorder themselves.

Have students write the time order words on self-stick notes and attach them to their Sequence Charts from last week. Have students echo-read their events using the time order words.

W.1.3 Write narratives in which they recount two or more appropriately sequenced events, include some details regarding what happened, use temporal words to signal event order, and provide some sense of closure. **W.1.5** With guidance and support from adults, focus on a topic, respond to questions and suggestions from peers, and add details to strengthen writing as needed. **L.1.1g** Use frequently occurring conjunctions (e.g., and, but, or, so, because). **L.1.1j** Produce and expand complete simple and compound declarative, interrogative, imperative, and exclamatory sentences in response to prompts.

Personal Narrative: Revise to Add Descriptive Details (10 MIN.) W.1.3, W.1.5, L.1.1g, L.1.1j

Student Objectives

I will be able to:
- Add descriptive details to my personal narrative draft.
- Use conjunctions in compound sentences.

Additional Materials

- Writing portfolios
- Personal Narrative Draft (from Day 1)

Presentation BLM 28
- Conjunctions Chart

Engage Thinking

Display your personal narrative draft from yesterday.

Say: *Today we will look more closely at our personal narrative drafts and add details to the descriptions. Think about the setting and events in your narrative. Remember that descriptions that use words that appeal to the senses–sight, hearing, touch, taste, and smell–help readers visualize what is being described.*

Model

Work with students to revise your personal narrative draft. Explain that you will add more details to your writing to help readers visualize where the story takes place and what happens to the characters. As you write each sentence, model how you apply your knowledge of print concepts, phonics, high-frequency words, and English language conventions.

The Day I Slept Late

I was excited to go fishing with grandpa at blue lake. First, grandpa helped me set the clock for 6:00. Then I went to sleep. I woke up and I saw the green numbers on my clock. It was 8:00 and the house was quiet. The alarm did not go off! Finally, I checked the clock. We had set the alarm for 6:00 at night! I learned that we should pay close attention when setting an alarm for something important.

Sample Personal Narrative Draft

Practice (iELD)

Have students work with their partner and read their own personal narrative drafts. Students should help their partners look for places where more detail, especially sensory detail, could improve their narrative.

Independent Writing

Say: *Now it's your turn to write. Think about what details you can add to the description of the setting or events in your story. Think about the way things looked, sounded, tasted, smelled, and felt.*

Students may revise during writer's workshop time or at a writing station during small-group reading time. Independent Writing should occur before the Partner Share. Use the Build Language Review as needed while you confer and monitor.

Confer and Monitor

As students revise independently, support their efforts as needed using prompts like those provided here.

Directive Feedback: *Think of the five senses: sight, hearing, touch, taste, and smell. Where in your story can you use any of these senses? Find a good place to add sensory detail.*

Self-Monitoring and Reflection: *Visualize the experience. What do you see and hear? How can you describe those sights and sounds for your reader?*

Validating and Confirming: *You've added several strong details. They really bring your narrative to life.*

Partner Share

Say: *Now let's share our drafts with partners. Read your draft out loud. Point out the details you've added to your story.*

Monitor partners as they share their writing. Remind students to put their draft in their Personal Narrative Portfolio.

Build Language Review: Use Conjunctions

Remind students that they have practiced using conjunctions **and, but, or, so,** and **because** to join two parts of a sentence.

Say: *Remember, the conjunction **and** joins two sentences. The conjunctions **or** and **but** show a difference. The conjunctions **because** and **so** tell why something happened.*

Display the following sentences. Ask students to suggest endings that can be added to complete each compound sentence.

> Rabbit hops through the forest because ___.
> Monkey wants to warn the animals, so ___.
> Lion King calls all the animals to a meeting, but ___.
> Mosquito can come our and speak, or ___.
> Mother Owl finds her baby, and ___.

Oral Language Practice

Have pairs take turns asking and answering the following questions. Instruct them to use the word in parenthesis in their responses: *Why does Rabbit hop through the forest? (because) How does Monkey warn the animals? (so) What two things might Mosquito do at the meeting? (or) What does Mother Owl do when she finds her baby? (and)*

Integrated ELD

Light Support
Display the pictures students draw or the quick writes students composed last week during the Brainstorm step of the writing process. Assist students as they brainstorm describing words for the picture or sentences in the quick write. Ask students to use the list of words to add details to the sentences in their drafts.

Moderate Support
Display the pictures students draw or the quick writes students composed last week during the Brainstorm step of the writing process. Encourage them to name color words or other describing words to go with the picture or quick write. Model how to add describing words to their drafts. Have students echo-read their new sentences.

Substantial Support
Display the pictures students draw or the quick writes students composed last week during the Brainstorm step of the writing process. Ask discussion questions that will help students describe their pictures. For example: *What color is this? What sound did this animal make? Where did you go?* If needed, provide choices for answers: *What color is this, blue or green?* Model how to add describing words to their drafts. Have students echo-read their new sentences.

W.1.3 Write narratives in which they recount two or more appropriately sequenced events, include some details regarding what happened, use temporal words to signal event order, and provide some sense of closure. **W.1.5** With guidance and support from adults, focus on a topic, respond to questions and suggestions from peers, and add details to strengthen writing as needed. **L.1.1g** Use frequently occurring conjunctions (e.g., and, but, or, so, because). **L.1.1j** Produce and expand complete simple and compound declarative, interrogative, imperative, and exclamatory sentences in response to prompts.

Personal Narrative: Edit for Capitalization (10 MIN.) W.1.3, W.1.5, L.1.1j, L.1.2a

Engage Thinking

Display your personal narrative draft from Day 2. Remind students that this is your revised draft. Tell students that now they are going to edit their drafts by looking carefully for errors in capitalization. Go over the basic rules for capitalization:

- The first letter of the first word in a sentence should be capitalized.
- The first letter of the first word in spoken dialogue should be capitalized.
- Proper nouns, like the names of people and places, should be capitalized. If somebody has a title as part of their name, such as Dr. Williams, the first letter of the title gets capitalized.
- Months of the year and days of the week should be capitalized.
- Titles of books, television shows, and movies should be capitalized.

Model

Display your edits and discuss the changes you made.

- *Blue Lake is a proper noun, so I need to make the **b** in **blue** and the **l** in **lake** capital letters.*
- *This is tricky, but Grandpa is a proper noun too. Because I'm using it like a name— I call my grandfather "Grandpa"—it should get a capital **G** like it was a name.*

The Day I Slept Late

I was excited to go fishing with Grandpa at Blue Lake. First, Grandpa helped me set the clock for 6:00. Then I went to sleep. I woke up and I saw the green numbers on my clock. It was 8:00 and the house was quiet. The alarm did not go off! Finally, I checked the clock. We had set the alarm for 6:00 at night! I learned that we should pay close attention when setting an alarm for something important.

Sample Personal Narrative Draft

Practice

Have students work with partners to edit their drafts and identify places where they need to fix the capitalization. Tell students that working with a partner is a great way to help improve their draft: a reader can often catch mistakes the writer does not see. Monitor students and assist them with the rules of capitalization, as necessary.

Independent Writing

Say: *Now it's your turn to edit your draft. Read your personal narrative draft aloud and correct the capitalization. This is your last round of changes, so make your writing the strongest it can be.*

Students may edit during writer's workshop time or at a writing station during small-group reading time. Independent Writing should occur before the Partner Share. Use the Build Language Review as needed while you confer and monitor.

Student Objectives

I will be able to:
- Edit my personal narrative draft to check and correct capitalization.
- Identify and produce different kinds of sentences.

Additional Materials

- Writing portfolios
Presentation BLM 29
- Sentences Chart

Confer and Monitor

As students edit independently, support their efforts as needed using prompts like those provided here.

Directive Feedback: *Use the capitalization rules we discussed as a checklist and use that to help guide your edits.*

Self-Monitoring and Reflection: *Are there any words in your writing that you feel unsure about capitalizing? What are they?*

Validating and Confirming: *Great work! You did a careful job editing.*

Partner Share

Say: *Now let's share our edited drafts with partners. Read your draft out loud. Point out what changes you made and why you made each change.*

Monitor partners as they share their writing. Remind students to put their edited draft in their Personal Narrative Portfolio.

Build Language Review: Use Simple and Compound Sentences (iELD)

Remind students that there are different kinds of sentences: declarative, interrogative, imperative, exclamatory. These different kinds of sentences can be simple sentences or compound sentences.

Display the following chart. Complete the chart with your students. Think of two sample sentences for each sentence type: a simple sentence and a compound sentence.

Kind of Sentence	What It Does	End Mark	Sample Sentences
Declarative	makes a statement	.	Simple: Bill had to go on a business trip. Compound: Sarah went to school, and she brought her lunch.
Imperative	gives a command	.	
Interrogative	asks a question		
Exclamatory			

Oral Language Practice

Have pairs find different kinds of sentences in *Why Mosquitoes Buzz in People's Ears*. Have them read a sentence aloud, identify the end mark, and use the Sentence Chart from the Build Language Review to identify what kind of sentence it is, what it does, and whether it is a simple or compound sentence.

(iELD) Integrated ELD

Light Support
Have student pairs write, punctuate, share, and discuss correctly punctuated sentences.
Oh, it might be dark for the rest of time ___ (!)
Did you call the sun ___ (?)
Find my baby, please ___ (.)
Mother Owl is sad ___ (.)

Moderate Support
Review the Sentence Chart from Build Language Review. Explain the different kinds of sentences and their end punctuation.
Then have groups write, punctuate, and share correctly punctuated sentences.
Oh, it is so dark ___ (!)
Monkey is to blame ___ (.)
Tell us, Crow ___ (.)
Is that Mother Owl ___ (?)

Substantial Support
Review the Sentence Chart from Build Language Review. Explain the different kinds of sentences and their end punctuation.
Write these sentences on the board:
Oh, I found Owlet ___ (!)
Tell us, Monkey ___ (.)
Mother Owl sat ___ (.)
Where is the sun ___ (?)
As a group, determine the correct end punctuation for each sentence.

W.1.3 Write narratives in which they recount two or more appropriately sequenced events, include some details regarding what happened, use temporal words to signal event order, and provide some sense of closure. **W.1.5** With guidance and support from adults, focus on a topic, respond to questions and suggestions from peers, and add details to strengthen writing as needed. **L.1.1j** Produce and expand complete simple and compound declarative, interrogative, imperative, and exclamatory sentences in response to prompts. **L.1.2a** Capitalize dates and names of people.

Publish the Personal Narrative (10 MIN.)

W.1.3, W.1.6, L.1.1g, L.1.1j

Engage Thinking

Remind students that in the last two weeks, you have been working together to write personal narratives. Display and reread your mentor text. When you finish, spend a few moments reviewing the processes you went through to plan, draft, revise, and edit your personal narrative.

The Day I Slept Late

I was excited to go fishing with Grandpa at Blue Lake. First, Grandpa helped me set the clock for 6:00. Then I went to sleep. I woke up and I saw the green numbers on my clock. It was 8:00 and the house was quiet. The alarm did not go off! Finally, I checked the clock. We had set the alarm for 6:00 at night! I learned that we should pay close attention when setting an alarm for something important.

Mentor Personal Narrative

Say: *Today we will publish our personal narratives. I published my narrative by typing it on a word processing program on a computer. You can also publish your narrative by writing a neat, final copy.*

Create a Publishing Checklist

Say: *Let's make a chart to show what our published personal narratives should include.*

Feature	Digital Publication	Handwritten
title at top		
author's name under title		
darker font for title and author	X	
clear handwriting		X
correct spacing		
add a drawing (optional)		

Publishing Checklist

Peer Collaboration

Have students read their final draft aloud to a partner and decide how they're going to publish their personal narrative.

Student Objectives

I will be able to:
• Correct my draft to create a final version of my personal narrative.
• Identify and use conjunctions in compound sentences.

Additional Materials

• Writing portfolios
Presentation BLM 30
• Publishing Checklist

Publication

Students may publish during writer's workshop time or at a writing station during small-group reading time. Remind students to put their published piece in their Personal Narrative Portfolio.

Build Language Review: Use Simple and Compound Sentences (iELD)

Remind students that they have been using conjunctions to join simple sentences and create compound sentences.

Ask students to identify conjunctions in their personal narrative. Have them identify what each conjunction does.

Oral Language Practice

Have pairs discuss how their personal narratives are alike and different. Have them produce compound sentences that compare and contrast their narratives using conjunctions **and, but, so,** and **because.** Have each pair share their sentences with the group.

Integrated ELD

Light Support
Have students work with a partner to compare and contrast digital versus handwritten publication. Tell students to focus on the benefits and drawbacks of each. Have students create their own Comparison-Contrast Chart to help them organize their thoughts. After partners have had a chance to discuss, have pairs share their ideas with the class. Take the opportunity to discuss terms that students might not be fully familiar with, like **font.**

Moderate Support
Work with students to create a Comparison-Contrast Chart for the benefits and drawbacks of digital and handwritten publication. Take the opportunity to discuss terms that students might not be fully familiar with, like **font.**

Substantial Support
Use your mentor text to illustrate each item in the digital column of the Publishing Checklist. Working with students, place a number next to the item in the checklist. Then number the appropriate feature in your mentor text with the same number. Take the opportunity to discuss terms and features that students might not be fully familiar with.

W.1.3 Write narratives in which they recount two or more appropriately sequenced events, include some details regarding what happened, use temporal words to signal event order, and provide some sense of closure. **W.1.6** With guidance and support from adults, use a variety of digital tools to produce and publish writing, including in collaboration with peers. **L.1.1g** Use frequently occurring conjunctions (e.g., and, but, or, so, because). **L.1.1j** Produce and expand complete simple and compound declarative, interrogative, imperative, and exclamatory sentences in response to prompts.

Share Personal Narratives (10 MIN.) W.1.3, SL.1.1a

Student Objectives

I will be able to:
• Share my personal narrative with a partner.
• Compliment, question, and make suggestions on a partner's personal narrative.

Additional Materials

• Writing portfolios

Engage Thinking

Display and read the published copy of your personal narrative.

> **The Day I Slept Late**
> by _____
> I was excited to go fishing with Grandpa at Blue Lake. First, Grandpa helped me set the clock for 6:00. Then I went to sleep. I woke up and I saw the green numbers on my clock. It was 8:00 and the house was quiet. The alarm did not go off! Finally, I checked the clock. We had set the alarm for 6:00 at night! I learned that we should pay close attention when setting an alarm for something important.

Mentor Personal Narrative

Say: *During the past two weeks, we have learned many steps writers take when they work. We brainstormed ideas. We planned our writing. We wrote a draft and then revised and edited the draft to strengthen our writing. Finally, we published our writing. Now we are ready to share our published writing with others. We're going to practice our three sharing skills: giving a compliment, asking a question, and offering a suggestion.*

Model Peer Collaboration (IELD)

Read aloud your published personal narrative. Then ask a volunteer to introduce his or her narrative and read it aloud. After reading, model how you give the writer a compliment using a sentence frame such as:

• *I like how you _____ because it helped me _____.*
• *My favorite part was _____ because _____.*
• *It was really interesting when _____ and I liked that because _____.*

Remind students that compliments can be about any part of the writing, but they should always describe something positive and point to something specific. Point out that your compliment is kind and specific.

Allow partners to read their narratives and give each other compliments.

Next, model asking questions. Return to your student-partner's narrative and model asking questions with sentence frames such as:

• *When we were brainstorming topics, how did you decide on _____?*
• *What revision do you think made the biggest difference to your writing?*
• *What was the hardest part of your writing?*
• *What is your favorite part of your narrative?*

Point out that questions can be about the details in the writer's work or about the how the writer created his or her narrative. Either way, the questions should be friendly and focus on an important aspect of the narrative.

Allow students time to ask their partner questions.

Finally, model offering a suggestion. Return to your student-partner's narrative and model offering your partner a suggestion to improve his or her writing. Use the following samples to help craft a suggestion.

- *I was a little confused by the order of events at the end of the story. Maybe using some signal words would help your reader follow the story.*
- *The section about _____ would be a great place to add some strong sensory words to the description.*
- *I would love to hear more details about _____. That section was really interesting and I wanted to know more.*

Explain to students that suggestions must be kind, specific to the work, and helpful to the writer. Review your own modeled suggestion and point out how it meets this criteria.

Allow time for students to review their partner's work and offer suggestions.

Practice Peer Collaboration

Invite partners to read their published personal narratives out loud and give compliments, ask questions, and make suggestions about each other's work. Remind them that the writer should respond by saying "Thank you" and/or answering the question.

Whole-Group Share

Select a few students to share their personal narratives with the whole group. Invite class members to give compliments, ask questions, and make suggestions about each student's work.

Place the personal narratives in your classroom library for students to reread throughout the rest of the school year. Alternatively, allow students to take their portfolios home and/ or file them to use as documentation of students' developing writing skills.

Integrated ELD

Light Support
Have partners take turns reading the Mentor Personal Narrative aloud. Then have them give compliments that tell the parts of the story they like best.

Moderate Support
Have students echo-read the Mentor Personal Narrative. Have students give compliments about the text. Encourage them to use the following sentence frames:
I like ___.
I notice ___.

Substantial Support
Have students echo-read the Mentor Personal Narrative. Assist students in giving compliments about the text. Encourage them to use sentence frames such as *I like ___.*

W.1.3 Write narratives in which they recount two or more appropriately sequenced events, include some details regarding what happened, use temporal words to signal event order, and provide some sense of closure. **SL.1.1a** Follow agreed-upon rules for discussions (e.g., listening to others with care, speaking one at a time about the topics and texts under discussion).

Read an Informational Mentor Text

(10 MIN.) W.1.2

Engage Thinking

Explain that for the next two weeks, you will work together to write an informational text.

Say: *An informational text gives facts about a topic. It include facts and does not include imaginary details invented by the writer.*

Read the Mentor Text

Display and read aloud the following mentor text. When you finish, allow students to respond with comments or questions.

> **Dogs Are Special**
> **by Mrs. Smith**
> Many people have dogs as pets. Some dogs are big, and others are small.
> Dogs eat meat and plants. Most dog foods contain both. Dogs should be walked every day. This gives them exercise and prevents them from getting bored. Dogs need training on basic commands such as "sit," "down," and "stay." Good training helps dogs learn how to behave. You can show dogs you love them by petting them and giving them rewards. Dogs make great pets when you care for them properly!

Informational Mentor Text

Analyze the Mentor Text

Say: *Let's use this text to analyze the parts, or features, of an informational text.*

As you go through the Informational Mentor Text, point out the following features and list them on a chart:

> **An informational text has:**
> • a title and an author
> • a topic
> • an introduction
> • facts
> • a conclusion

Informational Text Anchor Chart

 Quick Write and Share

Say: *Let's do a quick write. You will have five minutes to write a true-life topic you care about. Write about facts you know are true. Do not tell a story or invent details.*

Explain to students that this activity will prepare them for a longer informational writing assignment they will do later this week. When students finish, ask them to share their work with a partner.

Student Objectives

I will be able to:
• Identify the features of an informational text.
• Read and analyze a mentor text.
• Use singular and plural nouns with matching verbs.

Additional Materials

• Writing portfolios
Presentation BLM 31
• Nouns and Matching Verbs Chart

Present Portfolios

Hand out prepared portfolios. These can be as simple as manila file folders labeled "Informational Text."

Say: *Here is a portfolio you may use to store all the writing you do for the next two weeks. Storing your writing papers in your portfolio will help you organize your work and ideas so you can look back at your papers whenever you like.*

Allow time for students to write their names on their portfolios, file their quick writes, and store the portfolios in a designated spot in the classroom.

Build Language Review: Singular and Plural Nouns  (10 MIN.) L.1.1c

Remind students that a noun names a person, place, or thing, and that some nouns tell about more than one. Also remind them that a verb describes the action. A verb can tell the action of one or more persons or things.

Say: *Remember that the noun and the verb in a sentence must match. If the noun is singular, the verb must be singular. If the noun is plural, the verb must be plural.*

Display the chart below. Lead students in revising each sentence so the verb matches with the noun.

Unmatched Nouns and Verbs	Matched Nouns and Verbs
The girl help.	[The girl helps.]
The boys sings.	[The boys sing.]
My uncle walk to work.	[My uncle walks to work.]
The children plays soccer.	[The children play soccer.]

Nouns and Matching Verbs Chart

Oral Language Practice

Have partners say additional sentences with correct noun-verb agreement. For example: *My mom drives a blue car; Joe rides his bike; Samantha drinks water.*

Light Support

Say: *We use different verbs for singular and plural nouns.*

Ask students to generate sentences using the correct verb to accompany these nouns: **My sister, Mr. Bradshaw, the twins, the kittens, the books.**

Moderate Support

Say: *We use different verbs for singular and plural nouns.*

Draw the chart below on the board. Ask students to come up to the board and circle the correct verb.

Nouns	Verbs	
Mom and Dad	drive	drives
Raccoons	live	lives
My dog	play	plays
The White House	has	have

Substantial Support

Say: *We use different verbs for singular and plural nouns.*

Write these sentences on the board:

Mom and Dad drive the car.

Joe drives the car, too.

Ask: *Is the noun singular or plural? What happens when the noun is singular?* (add an **s**) *What happens when the noun is plural?*

W.1.2 Write informative/explanatory texts in which they name a topic, supply some facts about the topic, and provide some sense of closure. **L.1.1c** Use singular and plural nouns with matching verbs in basic sentences (e.g., He hops; We hop).

© Benchmark Education Company, LLC

Grade 1 • Unit 7 • Week 2 **63**

Informational Text: Brainstorm

(10 MIN.) W.1.2, L.1.1c

Engage Thinking

Display the Informational Text Anchor Chart you created on Day 1.

Say: *Now we will brainstorm topics for our informational text. While we brainstorm, let's keep the anchor chart in mind. We want to think of topics that help us create all the things we know a strong informational text must have.*

Model

Use a think-aloud to model generating a list of possible informational text topics. Encourage students to focus on topics they like and know well.

Sample think-aloud: *An informational text tells about a specific topic. That topic must be something from real life. The details we include in our writing will be facts about our topic. It will be helpful if I write about something I really understand. That way, I'll have a lot of details I can include. Let me think about topics I know a lot about.*

Create a topic list. For example:

Topic Ideas
1. Planning basketball
2. Taking care of a pet dog
3. Baking bread

Sample think-aloud: *Now I'll look at the list I created. What topic is something I would like writing about and is something I know about? I think I'll write about dogs. I have a pet dog and I help take care of it.*

Practice (iELD)

Say: *Turn and talk to your partner about topics you might want to write about. As you think of topics, explain to your partner why you think the topic is a good one. You can also tell your partner what would be challenging about the topic. Remember to listen to your partner as they share their ideas with you.*

 Quick Write

Say: *Now it's your turn to brainstorm ideas. You have five minutes to write a list of topics you could use for your informational writing. When you finish, review your list and draw a star next to the topic you want to write about. Then put your completed list in your Informational Text Portfolio.*

Student Objectives

I will be able to:
• Brainstorm a list of topics for an informational text.
• Use singular and plural nouns with matching verbs.

Additional Materials

• Writing portfolios
Presentation BLM 32
• Nouns and Matching Verbs Chart

Build Language Review: Singular and Plural Nouns

Remind students that they have learned how to match singular and plural nouns to verbs.

Say: *Remember that the noun and the verb in a sentence must match. A singular noun and verb go together, and a plural noun and verb go together.*

Display the chart below. Lead students in writing the plural nouns and matching verbs for each phrase.

Singular Nouns and Matching Verbs	Plural Nouns and Matching Verbs
student eats	[students eat]
teacher tells	[teachers tell]
ball bounces	[balls bounce]
dog runs	[dogs run]

Nouns and Matching Verbs Chart

Oral Language Practice

Have partners say additional phrases with the correct noun-verb agreement. For example: *student works, students work; cat meows, cats meow; ship sails, ships sail.*

Integrated ELD

Light Support

Have students work with a partner to think of topic ideas for their informational text. Have students make a list of their ideas and talk with their partner about which idea is best.

Moderate Support

Have students work with a partner to think of topic ideas for their informational text. Remind students that they should think of topics that they already know about. Provide a sentence frame to help them brainstorm.

I can write about _____ because I know _____.

Substantial Support

Have students work with a partner. Ask them to talk about animals that they like and to tell what they know about each animal. Provide sentence frames to help them brainstorm.

I like _____. It has _____. It lives in _____.

W.1.2 Write informative/explanatory texts in which they name a topic, supply some facts about the topic, and provide some sense of closure. **L.1.1c** Use singular and plural nouns with matching verbs in basic sentences (e.g., He hops; We hop).

Informational Text: Planning (10 MIN.) W.1.2, L.1.1c

Engage Thinking

Display the Informational Text Anchor Chart from Day 1 and review it with students.

Say: *A strong informational text has a clear topic and gives readers facts that help explain the topic. It also has an introduction and a conclusion. Today we will plan our writing by deciding what facts we need to include in our informational writing.*

Model

Use a think-aloud to model how to plan an informational text.

Sample think-aloud: *We have brainstormed topics for our informational texts. I am going to write about dogs. Now I will plan my writing. I will write the big ideas I know about dogs and the supporting facts for each idea. I am going to use a planning chart to organize the key ideas and facts my informational text will present.*

Model filling out the Planning Chart with your class. Begin by modeling the selection of key ideas. Then write down the first two or three ideas and facts, then collaborate with your class to complete the planning chart.

• *When I plan, I write the topic of my informational text and the key ideas.*
• *Next, I write down the facts that support each idea. I don't worry about writing complete sentences. I just want to get my ideas written down on paper.*

Topic: Dogs	
Key Ideas	**Facts**
Dogs are different sizes.	• Some are big • Some are small • The size depends on the breed
Dogs eat meat and plants.	• They can eat different kinds of meat and fish • They eat some plants • Dog food usually has a mixture of meat and plants
Dogs need exercise.	• They should be walked every day • Exercise prevents dogs from getting bored
Dogs need love.	• They should be petted and played with • They should be rewarded when they behave • They are part of the family

Sample Informational Text Planning Chart

Practice (IELD)

Distribute planning charts to the students. Have students work with a partner to complete the first step of the planning process: selecting key ideas. Remind students to listen to their partners' ideas and provide feedback that will help their partners plan their informational text. Have students write their key ideas into their planning charts. Tell students that this plan will help them during the writing process.

 **Quick Write**

Say: *Now it's your turn to write. Complete your plan by adding facts about the topic you chose. Remember, you do not need to write these facts as complete sentences. This is just the plan, and the important thing is to get all the facts you need in the places you need them.*

When students complete their plans, have them add the plan to their Informational Text Portfolio.

Build Language Review: Singular and Plural Nouns with Matching Verbs

Remind students that they have learned that some nouns tell about more than one person or thing.

Say: *Remember that a verb tells what the noun does in a sentence. It is important that the noun and verb match.*

Display the chart below. Lead students in writing the plural nouns and matching verbs for each phrase.

Singular Nouns and Matching Verbs	Plural Nouns and Matching Verbs
diagram shows	[diagrams show]
computer helps	[computers help]
artist illustrates	[artists illustrate]
time line shows	[time lines show]

Nouns and Matching Verbs Chart

Oral Language Practice
Have partners say additional phrases with the correct noun-verb agreement. For example: *rabbit hops, rabbits hop; cheetah runs, cheetahs run; bird flies, birds fly.*

 Integrated ELD

Light Support
Give students note cards that they can use to write down the facts they will present in their informational texts. Have students write one big idea on each card, then work with a partner to write supporting facts for each big idea on the other side of each card.

Moderate Support
Give students note cards that they can use to write down the facts for their informational texts. Write this sentence frame on each note card:
The first big idea is _____.
Students should complete the sentence frame and then write supporting facts for that big idea on the back of the card.

Substantial Support
Give students note cards that they can use to write the facts for their informational texts. On the front of each index card, write this sentence frame:
The first big idea is _____.
On the back of each index card, write this sentence frame: *One fact is _____.*
Ask students to complete each sentence frame.

W.1.2 Write informative/explanatory texts in which they name a topic, supply some facts about the topic, and provide some sense of closure. **L.1.1c** Use singular and plural nouns with matching verbs in basic sentences (e.g., He hops; We hop).

Informational Text: Writing a Draft

(10 MIN.) W.1.2, L.1.1c

Engage Thinking

Tell students that now that they have completed their planning, it is time to use their plans to help them write a draft of their informational text.

Say: *Let's review our planning chart before we begin.*

Topic: Dogs	
Key Ideas	**Facts**
Dogs are different sizes.	• Some are big • Some are small • The size depends on the breed
Dogs eat meat and plants.	• They can eat different kinds of meat and fish • They eat some plants • Dog food usually has a mixture of meat and plants
Dogs need exercise.	• They should be walked every day • Exercise prevents dogs from getting bored
Dogs need love.	• They should be petted and played with • They should be rewarded when they behave • They are part of the family

Sample Informational Text Planning Chart

Model

Work with students to write a draft of your informational text. Point out that the draft should open with a statement of your most important idea. Show how the key ideas and supporting facts from the Planning Chart form the following sentences. As you write each sentence, model how you apply your knowledge of print concepts, phonics, high-frequency words, and English language conventions. Note that the draft contains intentional errors in spelling that will be corrected in the editing step of the writing process.

> Many people have dogs as pets. Some dogs are big, and others are small.
> Dogs eat meet and plants. Most dog foods contan both. Dogs should be walked every day. This gives them exercise and prevents them from getting bored.
> You can show dogs you love them by petting them and giving them rewards.

Sample Informational Text Draft

Practice

Say: *Now turn to a partner and discuss how you will start your essay and what facts you will include to support your key ideas. Work together to help each other pick the strongest facts. Listen to your partner and give them feedback to help them make their draft as strong as it can be.*

Additional Materials

• Writing portfolios
Presentation BLM 35
• Nouns and Matching Verbs Chart

Independent Writing

Provide time for students to write independently.

Students may write during writer's workshop time or at a writing station during small-group reading time. Independent Writing should occur before the Partner Share. Use the Build Language Review as needed while you confer and monitor.

 **Confer and Monitor**

As students write independently, support their efforts as needed using prompts like those provided here.

Directive Feedback: *Use your planning chart to keep you on track. Follow your plan!*

Self-Monitoring and Reflection: *Did you think of ways to change your plan as you wrote? How do you think these changes would improve your writing?*

Validating and Confirming: *Excellent draft! You introduction is clear and your facts support your key ideas.*

Partner Share

Say: *Now let's share our drafts with a partner. While we share, let's practice our sharing skills: giving compliments, asking questions, and offering suggestions.*

Select a student as your partner and model one sharing skill. Monitor partners as they share their drafts and provide feedback. After students are done sharing, have them place their drafts in their Informational Text portfolios.

Build Language Review: Singular and Plural Nouns with Matching Verbs

Say: *Remember that a noun is a person, place, or thing. A verb tells what the noun does. It is important that the noun and verb match in a sentence.*

Display the chart below. Lead students in completing each sentence with the correct form of the verb that matches the noun.

Sentence Frame	Verbs	Completed Sentence
The Native Americans _____ hard.	work/works	[The Native Americans work hard.]
A dentist _____ my teeth.	clean/cleans	[A dentist cleans my teeth.]
The Taj Mahal _____ nice.	look/looks	[The Taj Mahal looks nice.]
The parrots _____ loudly.	whistle/whistles	[The parrots whistle loudly.]

Nouns and Matching Verbs Chart

Oral Language Practice

Have partners say additional sentences with the correct noun-verb agreement. For example: *The geese fly south for the winter.*

Integrated ELD

Light Support
Review verbs for singular and plural nouns. Ask students to write sentences using the correct verb to accompany these nouns: **George Washington, Native Americans, ships, soldier.**

Moderate Support
Review verbs for singular and plural nouns. Display this chart. Ask students to circle the correct verb.

Natives	hunt	hunts
Settlers	farm	farms
The wind	blow	blows
Plant	grow	grows
The sun	shine	shines

Substantial Support
Say: *We use different verbs for singular and plural nouns.*
Read the sentences:
They build cabins of wood.
Their leader builds his home of wood, too.
Ask: *Is the noun singular or plural? What happens to the verb when the noun is singular? (add an* **s***) What happens when the noun is plural?*

W.1.2 Write informative/explanatory texts in which they name a topic, supply some facts about the topic, and provide some sense of closure. **L.1.1c** Use singular and plural nouns with matching verbs in basic sentences (e.g., He hops; We hop).

Informational Text: Write a Title and a Conclusion (10 MIN.) W.1.2, L.1.1c

Engage Thinking

Tell students that they have written most of their draft, but today they need to add a conclusion to their informational text. Tell them that they will also be writing a title. A strong title gives the reader an idea of what they are about to read.

Model

Model adding a title and a strong ending that captures the most important idea of your informational text and retells the idea in a new way. As you write each sentence, model how you apply your knowledge of print concepts, phonics, high-frequency words, and English language conventions. Note that the draft contains intentional errors in spelling that will be corrected in the editing step of the writing process.

> Dogs Are Special
>
> Many people have dogs as pets. Some dogs are big, and others are small.
> Dogs eat meet and plants. Most dog foods contan both.
> Dogs should be walked every day. This gives them exercise and prevents them from getting bored. You can show dogs you love them by petting them and giving them rewards. Dogs make great pets if you care for them praporly!

Sample Informational Text Draft

Oral Rehearsal for Independent Writing (iELD)

Invite partners to read their drafts out loud and work together to develop a title and a strong conclusion. Suggest that students think of several ideas for a title and pick their favorite.

Independent Writing

Say: *Now it's your turn to add to your draft. Write your own conclusion and title for your informational text.*

Students may write during writer's workshop time or at a writing station during small-group reading time. Independent Writing should occur before the Partner Share and Build Language Review.

Student Objectives

I will be able to:
• Write a title for an informational text.
• Write a conclusion for an informational text.
• Use singular and plural nouns with matching verbs.

Additional Materials

• Writing portfolios
Presentation BLM 36
• Nouns and Matching Verbs Chart

 ## Confer and Monitor

As students write independently, support their efforts as needed using prompts like those provided here.

Directive Feedback: *What is your most important idea? How can you say that in another way? That is your new conclusion!*

Self-Monitoring and Reflection: *Read your draft again. Does it show how much you like the topic you chose? How can you make the reader as interested in your topic as you are?*

Validating and Confirming: *Good work! Your title really expresses what your writing is about and your conclusion provides a satisfying ending.*

Partner Share

Say: *Now let's share our writing with a partner. Read your writing aloud. Talk with your partner about your conclusion and your title.*

Monitor partners as they share their writing.

Build Language Review: Singular and Plural Nouns with Matching Verbs

Remind students that the noun and verb in a sentence need to agree. A singular noun should be paired with a singular verb, and a plural noun goes with a plural verb.

Display the chart below. Lead students in rewriting each sentence so the nouns and verbs match.

Incorrect Sentence	Correct Sentence
The schools opens at 8:00.	[The schools open at 8:00.]
The glass fall on the floor.	[The glass falls on the floor.]
A duck quack loudly.	[A duck quacks loudly.]
A dog catch the ball.	[A dog catches the ball.]

Nouns and Matching Verbs Chart

Oral Language Practice
Have partners say additional sentences with the correct noun-verb agreement. For example: *My friends play football. The students work hard. My sister turns 16 next week.*

 ## Integrated ELD

Light Support
Have students work with a partner. Give each pair note cards. Have them write ideas for their conclusion on the note cards and discuss why each idea is a good one.

Moderate Support
Have students work with a partner. Have them work together to write conclusion ideas. Give them sentence frames to help them express why an idea is a good one.
This is a good conclusion idea because _____.

Substantial Support
Have students work with a partner. Give them sentence frames to write conclusion ideas and to help them express why an idea is a good one.
One conclusion idea is _____.
This is a good conclusion idea because _____.

W.1.2 Write informative/explanatory texts in which they name a topic, supply some facts about the topic, and provide some sense of closure. **L.1.1c** Use singular and plural nouns with matching verbs in basic sentences (e.g., He hops; We hop).

Informational Text: Revise to Add More Facts (10 MIN.) W.1.2, L.1.1c

Engage Thinking

Display the first draft of your informational text. Remind students that a draft is not a finished piece of writing.

Say: *Now, we are going to revise our drafts by adding key facts to further develop the topic. Remember that when you revise, you focus on making your writing even stronger. You rewrite sentences to improve your text.*

Model

Work with students to revise your informational text draft. Model further developing the topic by adding new and important ideas and facts to your draft. Add one key idea and one fact that supports it. As you write each sentence, model how you apply your knowledge of print concepts, phonics, high-frequency words, and English language conventions. Note that the samples contains intentional spelling errors which will be corrected in the editing step of the writing process.

> **Dogs Are Special**
> Many people have dogs as pets. Some dogs are big, and others are small. Dogs eat meet and plants. Most dog foods contan both. Dogs should be walked every day. This gives them exercise and prevents them from getting bored.
> Dogs need traning on basic commands, such as *sit*, *down*, and *stay*.
> Good training helps dogs learn how to behave.
> You can show dogs you love them by petting them and giving them rewards.
> Dogs make great pets if you care for them praporly!

Sample Informational Text Draft

Practice

Now ask students to read their draft to a partner and discuss what key ideas and facts they might add to their writing. Remind students to listen to their partner and help them improve their writing. Each student should add at least one key idea, and one fact that supports it, to his or her draft.

Independent Writing

Say: *Now it's your turn to revise. Read your draft again. Add one key idea and one supporting fact to improve your writing.*

Students may write during writer's workshop time or at a writing station during small-group reading time. Independent Writing should occur before the Partner Share and Build Language Review.

Student Objectives

I will be able to:
• Add details about facts in an informational text.
• Use singular and plural nouns with matching verbs.

Additional Materials

• Writing portfolios
Presentation BLM 37
• Matching Nouns and Verbs Chart

Confer and Monitor

As students revise independently, support their efforts as needed using prompts like those provided here.

Directive Feedback: *Look back on your plan. Are there any key ideas or facts you didn't include in your initial draft? Could you use them now?*

Self-Monitoring and Reflection: *Try to recall what it was like first learning about your topic. What was hard to understand? That is probably a place where readers need help too. Add ideas and facts to explain whatever first gave you trouble.*

Validating and Confirming: *The new idea and supporting facts about _____ really strengthen your explanation of the topic. Good work!*

Partner Share

Say: *Now let's share our writing with a partner. Read your writing aloud. Talk with your partner about the sentences you added, and explain why you added them.*

Choose a student to act as your partner and model sharing your sample draft. Monitor partners as they share their writing. After students have shared, tell them to place their drafts in their Informational Text portfolio.

Build Language Review: Matching Nouns and Verbs (iELD)

Say: *Nouns and verbs need to match when we talk about things that are happening now, or in the present. Singular nouns and singular verbs go together. Plural nouns and plural verbs go together. Let's change some singular nouns and verbs to plural.*

Display the chart below. Lead students in rewriting each sentence to change the singular nouns and verbs to plural.

Singular Nouns and Verbs	Plural Nouns and Verbs
The boy visits the monument.	[The boys visit the monument.]
The memorial has a lot of visitors.	[The memorials have a lot of visitors.]
The building is famous.	[The buildings are famous.]
The citizen works hard.	[The citizens work hard.]

Sample Matching Nouns and Verbs Chart

Oral Language Practice

Have partners say additional sentences, first with singular nouns and verbs and then with plural nouns and verbs. For example: *My friend plays tennis. My friends play tennis. The cat purrs loudly. The cats purr loudly. The president leads the country. The presidents lead the country.*

Integrated ELD

Light Support
Review verbs for singular and plural nouns.
Ask students to generate sentences using the correct verb to accompany these nouns: **Memorials, Mount Rushmore, Minutemen, statue, the White House.**

Moderate Support
Review verbs for singular and plural nouns.
Draw this chart on the board:

A memorial _____ us remember the past.
help   helps
Each face _____ about 60 feet long.
is   are
The statue _____ the soldiers.
honor   honors

Ask students to circle the correct verb for each sentence.

Substantial Support
Say: *We use different verbs for singular and plural nouns.*
Read these sentences aloud:
Mount Rushmore is a monument.
Four images are carved on it.
Ask: *Is the noun singular or plural? What happens when the noun is singular?* (use **is**) *What happens when the noun is plural?* (use **are**)

W.1.2 Write informative/explanatory texts in which they name a topic, supply some facts about the topic, and provide some sense of closure. **L.1.1c** Use singular and plural nouns with matching verbs in basic sentences (e.g., He hops; We hop).

Informational Text: Revise to Add Visual Support (10 MIN.) W.1.2, L.1.1c

Engage Thinking

Display the latest draft of your informational text. Explain that visuals, such as photos, can help a reader understand the text.

Say: *We have revised our drafts. Now we will make a plan to add some photos to help support what we wrote. Then we will look for pictures we can use.*

Model

Work with students to create a plan to provide visual support for your draft. Create a chart that indicates what section of the text you want to support with a photograph. Then write down ideas for images that would help illustrate the ideas in the text.

Text	Image
Dogs should be walked every day. This gives them exercise and prevents them from getting bored.	Photo of a person walking a dog on a leash
Dogs need training on basic commands such as *sit*, *down*, and *stay*. Good training helps dogs learn how to behave.	Photo of a person training a dog how to sit

Sample Visual Support Planning Chart

After you create your planning chart, work with the class to brainstorm ways to gather the images you need. Strategies may include online image searches, cutting images from magazines, and taking your own photographs. Discuss the benefits and drawbacks of each strategy. Depending on the time and resources available, you may wish to specify the method all members of the class will use.

Practice (iELD)

Tell students to turn to their partner and discuss the images they would like to use to support their informational writing. Each student should select at least two images to support their writing.

Independent Writing

Say: *Now it's your turn to create a visual support plan.*

If you are going to have students search for visuals in class, tell students that they can search for images after they have completed their plan.

Students may create plans and find images during writer's workshop time or at a writing station during small-group reading time. Independent Writing should occur before the Partner Share and Build Language Review.

Student Objectives

I will be able to:
- Add visual support to an informational text.
- Use singular and plural nouns with matching verbs.

Additional Materials

- Writing portfolios
- Access to visual resources (see Classroom Management Note)

Presentation BLMs 38 and 39
- Visual Support Planning Chart
- Nouns and Matching Verbs Chart

Classroom Management Note:

The lesson requires students to supplement their informational writing with visuals. Students may do this by searching online, by cutting out images from a collection of magazines, or through any other appropriate method. Before beginning this mini-lesson, be sure students will have the access they need to visual resources.

Confer and Monitor

As students revise independently, support their efforts as needed using prompts like those provided here.

Directive Feedback: *Find the key details in your informational writing. These will be the details you want to illustrate for readers.*

Self-Monitoring and Reflection: *What did you have the hardest time describing or explaining in your writing? Could a picture help you make that idea clearer?*

Validating and Confirming: *Excellent plan! These visuals will really help me understand the text and make your writing more interesting.*

Partner Share

Say: *Now we'll share our plans/visuals with a partner. Let's practice the sharing skills we've learned and give our partner a compliment, ask a question about his or her plan/visuals, or offer them a suggestion.*

Select a student as your partner and model one of the sharing strategies: giving a compliment, asking a question, or offering a suggestion. Point out to students that your feedback is kind in tone, specific to the writing, and intended to help your partner improve his or her informational writing.

Monitor partners as they share their work. After students have finished sharing, have them place their plans and images in their Informational Text portfolios.

Build Language Review: Singular and Plural Nouns

Say: *Nouns and verbs need to match when we write and say sentences. Singular nouns and verbs match. Plural nouns and verbs match.*

Help students rewrite each sentence to change the singular nouns and verbs to plural.

Singular Nouns and Matching Verbs	Plural Nouns and Matching Verbs
The girl visits the memorial.	[The girls visit the memorial.]
The memorial honors the president.	[The memorials honor the president.]
The worker carves the memorial.	[The workers carve the memorial.]
The boy walks to school.	[The boys walk to school.]

Nouns and Matching Verbs Chart

Oral Language Practice

Have partners say additional sentences first with singular nouns and verbs and then with plural nouns and verbs.

Integrated ELD

Light Support
Have students choose visuals that will support their writing. Have students explain why they chose each image, and explain what part of their draft each image supports.

Moderate Support
Have students choose visuals that will support their writing. Have students explain why they chose one of the images, and point out what part of their draft that image supports.

Substantial Support
Have students choose visuals that will support their writing. Give students sentence frames they can use to explain why they chose one of the images and which part of their draft that image supports.
I chose this image because _____.
The image tells something about _____.

W.1.2 Write informative/explanatory texts in which they name a topic, supply some facts about the topic, and provide some sense of closure., **L.1.1c** Use singular and plural nouns with matching verbs in basic sentences (e.g., He hops; We hop).

Informational Text: Edit the Draft to Correct Spelling Errors (10 MIN.) W.1.2, L.1.1c

Engage Thinking

Display the latest draft of your informational text. Explain that it is important to edit the draft to fix any mistakes.

Say: *We have revised our drafts and found visuals to support our text. Now we will edit our revised drafts to fix any spelling mistakes. What strategies can we use to help us spell difficult words?*

Remind students that they can try to sound out difficult words, try using familiar spelling patterns, or look up the proper spelling in a resource, such as a dictionary.

Model

First, display your revisions and discuss the changes you made and why you made them.

- *When I edit my draft, I look at each sentence on its own. First, I see that I spelled **meat** incorrectly. I spelled it like "to be introduced to somebody" and not like the food. The next sentence has a error in too. **Contain** needs an **i** after the **a**.*

Work with students to identify and correct the misspellings of **training** and **properly.**

Dogs Are Special

Many people have dogs as pets. Some dogs are big, and others are small. Dogs eat meat and plants. Most dog foods contain both. Dogs should be walked every day. This gives them exercise and prevents them from getting bored.

Dogs need training on basic commands such as *sit, down,* and *stay.*

Good training helps dogs learn how to behave.

You can show dogs you love them by petting them and giving them rewards.

Dogs make great pets if you care for them properly!

Sample Informational Text Draft

Practice

Ask students to read their draft to their partners and identify spelling errors they need to correct.

Independent Writing

Say: *Now it's your turn to write. Edit your own informational text to fix any mistakes in capitalization or use of commas.*

Students may write during writer's workshop time or at a writing station during small-group reading time. Independent Writing should occur before the Partner Share and Build Language Review.

Student Objectives

I will be able to:
- Edit a draft of an informational text.
- Use singular and plural nouns with matching verbs.

Additional Materials

- Writing portfolios
Presentation BLM 40
- Possessive Nouns Chart

Confer and Monitor

As students edit independently, support their efforts as needed using prompts like those provided here.

Directive Feedback: *Read each sentence of the draft aloud, to yourself. Often you catch mistakes when reading your writing out loud.*

Self-Monitoring and Reflection: *Think about spelling words that always give you trouble. Are there any of those words in your essay? Think of the errors you commonly mistake and double check for those.*

Validating and Confirming: *I see that you corrected _____ and _____. That's careful editing and it really improves your writing. Good work!*

Partner Share

Say: *Now let's share our writing with a partner. Read your writing aloud. Talk with your partner about the edits you made and how they improved your writing.*

Monitor partners as they share their writing.

Build Language Review: Possessive Nouns

Review with students that they have learned how to write possessive nouns.

Say: *Remember that a noun names a person, place, or thing. A possessive noun tells who or what owns or has something. Let's use the noun **president** as an example. If we want to tell that the president has a family, how do we write **president** as a possessive noun to show this?* (president's family)

Lead students in changing nouns to possessive nouns to show ownership.

Nouns	Possessive Nouns
boy jacket	[boy's jacket]
girl hat	[girl's hat]
baby toy	[baby's toy]
Mom car	[Mom's car]
Dad bike	[Dad's bike]

Possessive Nouns Chart

Oral Language Practice

Have partners say additional possessive noun phrases. For example: *teacher's book; friend's ball; building's roof.*

iELD Integrated ELD

Light Support

Ask students to work with partners to find examples of possessive nouns in *Memorials and Historic Buildings* (pages 5, 9, and 15).

Then have the patterns work together to turn the sentences from the "Words to Think About" pages into sentences that contain possessive nouns. For example: *Abraham Lincoln was America's president.*

Moderate Support

Point out examples of possessive nouns from *Memorials and Historic Buildings* (pages 5, 9, and 15).

Then have students work with partners to complete the following sentence frames using possessive nouns.

• *Each _____ (state's) representatives and senators can be found in Congress.*
• *The White House is the _____ (president's) home.*
• *Betsy _____ (Ross's) home is a historic building.*

Substantial Support

Point out examples of possessive nouns from *Memorials and Historic Buildings:*

• *A historic building helps us learn about our country's past.*
• *Theodore Roosevelt helped preserve our nation's parks and forests.*
• *These buildings help us learn about our country's past.*

Have students echo-read the first sentence. Then point out the possessive noun and explain the function of the apostrophe **s**. Then have students echo-read the next two sentences. Work with students to find the possessive nouns.

W.1.2 Write informative/explanatory texts in which they name a topic, supply some facts about the topic, and provide some sense of closure. **L.1.1c** Use singular and plural nouns with matching verbs in basic sentences (e.g., He hops; We hop).

Publish the Informational Text

(10 MIN.) W.1.2, L.1.1b

Engage Thinking

Remind students that in the last two weeks, you have been working together to write informational texts. Display and reread the Informational Mentor Text. When you finish, spend a few moments reviewing the processes you went through to plan, draft, revise, and edit your informational text.

Student Objectives

I will be able to:
- Correct a draft of an informational text to create a final version.
- Use possessive nouns.

Additional Materials
- Writing portfolios

Presentation BLMs 41 and 42
- Publishing Checklist
- Possessive Nouns Chart

> **Dogs Are Special**
> **by Mrs. Smith**
> Many people have dogs as pets. Some dogs are big, and others are small. Dogs eat meat and plants. Most dog foods contain both. Dogs should be walked every day. This gives them exercise and prevents them from getting bored. Dogs need training on basic commands such as *sit*, *down*, and *stay*. Good training helps dogs learn how to behave. You can show dogs you love them by petting them and giving them rewards.
> Dogs make great pets when you care for them properly!

Sample Informational Text

Say: *This is the published version of the informational text I wrote about pet dogs. Notice that I published it on a computer. You can also publish your work by writing a neat, error-free final copy.*

Create a Publishing Checklist

Say: *Before you publish your work, let's make a publishing checklist that will help you make sure that your finished work has everything a published piece of writing should have.*

Work with students to create a publishing checklist for digital and handwritten publication. You may ignore the row for adding visual support depending on whether you asked students to execute their plans to add supporting photographs.

Feature	Computer	Handwritten
title at top		
author's name under title		
special font for title and author		
clear handwriting		
correct spacing		
supporting images (optional)		

Sample Publishing Checklist

Peer Collaboration (IELD)

Have students read their final drafts aloud to a partner and decide how they're going to publish their informational texts. Students should discuss the benefits and drawbacks of each form of publishing.

Publication

Students may publish during writer's workshop time or at a writing station during small-group reading time. Remind students to put their published pieces in their personal narrative portfolios.

Build Language Review: Possessive Nouns

Teach students how to indicate a possessive noun for plural nouns and singular nouns that end in **s**.

Say: *When a possessive noun is singular and ends in an **s**, then you follow the normal rule of adding an apostrophe **s**. When the possessive noun is a plural noun that ends in an **s**, add the apostrophe, but do not add the extra **s**. For example: The project **Jess** finished is **Jess's** project. The project the **students** finished is the **students'** project.*

Lead students in changing nouns to possessive nouns to show ownership.

Nouns	Possessive Nouns
teachers	[teachers']
class	[class's]
babies	[babies']
mothers	[mothers']
bus	[bus's]

Possessive Nouns Chart

Oral Language Practice

Have partners take turns thinking of plural possessive nouns. The first partner thinks of a word, then the second partner must use the word as a possessive noun in a sentence.

Integrated ELD

Light Support
Have students publish their informational texts. Give students a checklist for publishing and a template they can use to write their final copies. Have them keep the fully executed check list in their portfolios.

Moderate Support
Have students publish their informational texts. Give students a checklist for publishing and a template for writing that has labels for each piece of the text, such as *name, title, picture,* and *text.* Have them keep the fully executed check list in their portfolios.

Substantial Support
Have students publish their informational texts. Give students a template for writing that has labels for each piece of the text, such as *name, title, picture,* and *text.* Give students a model to follow that shows how to use the template. Have them keep the fully executed check list in their portfolios.

W.1.2 Write informative/explanatory texts in which they name a topic, supply some facts about the topic, and provide some sense of closure. **L.1.1b** Use common, proper, and possessive nouns.

Share Informational Texts (10 MIN.) W.1.2

Engage Thinking

Display and read the published copy of your informational text.

Dogs Are Special
by Mrs. Smith
Many people have dogs as pets. Some dogs are big, and others are small.
Dogs eat meat and plants. Most dog foods contain both. Dogs should be walked every day. This gives them exercise and prevents them from getting bored. Dogs need training on basic commands such as *sit*, *down*, and *stay*. Good training helps dogs learn how to behave. You can show dogs you love them by petting them and giving them rewards.
Dogs make great pets when you care for them properly!

Informational Mentor Text

Say: *During the past two weeks, we have gone through the many steps of the writing process. We brainstormed ideas and planned our writing. We created a draft. We revised our work and edited it. Finally, we published our writing. Now we are ready to share our writing with others. We are also going to practice giving writers feedback.*

Model Peer Collaboration (IELD)

Read aloud your published informational text. Then ask a volunteer to introduce and read aloud his or her work to you. After reading, model how you give the writer a compliment using sentence frames such as:

- *I liked how you _____.*
- *I thought that _____ really supported what you were saying.*
- *I understood _____ better because you _____.*
- *I enjoyed the part _____.*

Remind students that compliments should be specific to the writer's work. You want to point out exactly what you liked about his or her writing. Tell students that compliments should also be kind. The writers work hard on their work, so it is rude to make them feel bad about it.

Have students share their work with their partners and give students time to give each other compliments.

Additional Materials
- Writing portfolios
Weekly Presentation: Unit 7, Week 3
- Informational Mentor Text

Next, return to your volunteer partner and practice asking him or her a question. Remind students that, as with the compliment, it is important to be kind and specific. Tell students that the goal of asking questions is to get the writer to think about ways they can improve his or her work. After reading, model asking a question using the following sentence frames:

- *Out of all the topics your brainstormed, why did you pick this topic?*
- *What fact did you find most interesting about your topic?*
- *What do you think is the most challenging part of the writing process?*

Finally, model offering suggestions with your volunteer partner. Remind students that suggestions should be said in a nice way, should be specific, and are meant to help the writer improve his or her writing next they write. Use the following sentence stems to help you model offering suggestions:

- *_____ seems like a really important key idea, and I'd like to read more facts about it.*
- *I think _____ would help the readers understand how important these details are.*
- *You should _____ with the conclusion to let your readers understand how you feel about the topic.*

Practice Peer Collaboration

Invite students to read their published writing to their partners and practice the three sharing skills they have learned. Monitor students as share their writing and feedback.

Whole-Group Share

Select a few student volunteers to read their informational texts to the whole class. Invite classmates to give compliments, ask questions, and make suggestions. Remind them that the writer should respond by saying "Thank you" and/or answering the question.

Place the informational texts in your classroom library for students to reread throughout the school year. Alternatively, allow students to take their portfolios home or file them to use as documentation of their' developing writing skills.

Integrated ELD

Light Support
Discuss the following chart.

Revising and Editing a First Draft
Read Aloud - Listen
Meaning
Grammar
Read Aloud - Look
Sentence Structure
Grammar Rules

Ask partners to read their first drafts to each other. Have students give positive feedback as well as make suggestions to each other.
I like _____. You should _____.

Moderate Support
Discuss the chart from Light Support. Model how to give positive feedback as well as make suggestions to each other.
I like _____. You should _____.

Substantial Support
Write these words on cards: **drafting, editing, prewriting, publishing,** and **revising.**
Place them in random order. Ask students to place them in sequential order.
Display and discuss the chart from Light Support.
As a group, model revising and editing. Have students listen and look for ways to improve their writing.

ELD.PI.1.2, ELD.PI.1.10

W.1.2 Write informative/explanatory texts in which they name a topic, supply some facts about the topic, and provide some sense of closure.

Read an Opinion Mentor Text (10 MIN.) W.1.1, SL.1.2

Student Objectives

I will be able to:
• Identify the features of an opinion text.
• Read and analyze an opinion mentor text.
• Use correct verb tense to tell about the past.

Additional Materials

• Writing portfolios
•

Engage Thinking

Explain that for the next two weeks, you will work together to write opinion texts.

Say: *An opinion is what someone thinks or how a person feels about a topic. When you write an opinion text, you clearly state your opinion and provide reasons to support it by using facts, details, or examples. You can end your opinion text with a sentence that restates and summarizes your opinion.*

Read the Mentor Text

Display and read aloud the following mentor text. When you finish, allow students to respond with comments or questions.

> **Sky Watching**
> **by _____**
>
> We can see stars in the night sky. Stars are interesting to look at. One reason stars are interesting is because they form pictures in the night sky. Did you know that long ago people named the giant pictures they saw? I also enjoy watching the stars sparkle at night. As I look up at the sky, I notice large and smaller stars in different colors. The more we look at the stars, the more we can learn about the stars that light the night sky!

Opinion Mentor Text

Analyze the Mentor Text

Say: *Let's use this text to analyze the parts, or features, of an opinion text.*

As you go through the text, point out the following features and list them on a chart:

> An opinion text:
> • has a title and author
> • names a topic or book
> • states an opinion about the topic or book
> • states at least one reason for the opinion
> • has a closing sentence about the opinion

Opinion Text Anchor Chart

Quick Write and Share

Say: *Today we will do something called a quick write. You will have five minutes to draw or write an opinion about a topic or book. You may use the sentence frame "I like _____ because _____" or "I think _____ because _____". You can use the opinion anchor chart to help you.*

Explain that this activity is a warm-up for writing a longer opinion text later this week. When students finish, ask them to share their work with a partner.

Present Portfolios

Hand out prepared portfolios. These can be as simple as manila file folders labeled "Opinion Text."

Say: *Here is a portfolio you may use to store all the writing you do for the next two weeks. This will help you organize your work and ideas so you can look back at them whenever you like.*

Allow time for students to write their names on their portfolios, file their quick-writes, and store the portfolios in a designated spot in the classroom.

Partner Share

Say: *Now let's share our writing with partners. First, name the kind of writing we've been talking about. Then read your sentence out loud.*

Monitor partners as they share their writing. Have students use the Opinion Text Anchor Chart to focus their discussion. Students should discuss what they've learned about writing an opinion from reading the mentor text and looking at the anchor chart.

Build Language: Verb Tense

(10 MIN.) L.1.1e

Remind students that a verb is a word that describes an action, or what happens. Explain that we use different verbs for telling about things that happen in the past, present, and future. Explain that present tense tells about what is happening now.

- Use examples to tell about things that are happening in the classroom now. For example: *I talk to the class. We read a book. Jake sits in his seat.*
- Ask students to listen to sentences that contain past tense verbs. Ask them to raise their hands to say the sentence in the present tense.
    The dog ate his food.
    My mother drove me to school.
    The kitten jumped up on the chair.
    My sneakers were wet.

Oral Language Practice

Have partners take turns sharing what they saw in the sky yesterday. Remind them to use past tense verbs as they generate their oral sentences. For example: *A plane flew across the sky. Three fluffy clouds floated above my house.*

W.1.1 Write opinion pieces in which they introduce the topic or name the book they are writing about, state an opinion, supply a reason for the opinion, and provide some sense of closure. **SL.1.2** Ask and answer questions about key details in a text read aloud or information presented orally or through other media. **L.1.1e** Use verbs to convey a sense of past, present, and future (e.g., Yesterday I walked home; Today I walk home; Tomorrow I will walk home).

(iELD) Integrated ELD

Light Support
Say: *Verbs that tell about things that are happening right now are called present tense verbs.*
Display this chart:

In the Past	Right Now (Present)
ate	
ran	
jumped	

Ask students to write the present tense verbs on the chart and act them out.

Moderate Support
Say: *Verbs that tell about things that are happening right now are called present tense verbs.*
Write a list of present and past tense verbs on a chart. Ask students to identify present tense verbs and then act them out.

| ran look write |
| eat sat jumped |
| sang wave smile |

Substantial Support
Say: *Verbs that tell about things that are happening right now are called present tense verbs.*
Write present tense verbs on cards, placing them facedown. Ask a student to pick a card and act it out. Have other students guess the verb.
Sample cards: **eat, sleep, skip,** and **write.**

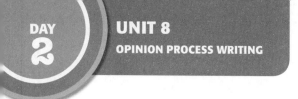
Opinion Text: Brainstorm (10 MIN.) W.1.1, SL.1.1, L.1.1e

Student Objectives

I will be able to:
• Brainstorm a list of topics to write about.
• Use correct verb tense to tell about the present.

Additional Materials

• Writing portfolios
Presentation BLM 43
• Opinion Chart

Engage Thinking

Remind students that when they brainstorm, they are coming up with ideas for what they want to write about. Yesterday, we read and discussed an opinion text about a favorite thing to look at in the sky.

Say: *Now I will think of ideas for a writing topic.*

Model

Use a think-aloud to model brainstorming ideas for a writing topic.

Sample think-aloud: *An opinion text tells what you think or how you feel about a topic. Before I write, I will brainstorm ideas. I ask myself, "What topics are interesting to me? What are my favorite things to think or talk about?" Usually, the topics I like are the topics I have an opinion about.*

Create an Opinion chart to record possible writing topics and your opinion about those topics. For example:

Topic	Opinion
Stars*	Stars are interesting to look at.
Birds	Birds are amazing.
Helicopters	Helicopters are useful air machines.

Sample Opinion Chart

Say: *Now I'll choose the topic I want to write about. I think I'd like to write about stars because they are interesting to look at. I'll put a star beside this topic.*

Practice

Say: *Turn and talk to your partner about a topic you would like to write about. Think about what makes your topic interesting and why you chose it. Make sure to state your opinion about the topic.*

 Quick Write

Say: *Now you will do a quick write. You will have five minutes to brainstorm ideas for your opinion text. You may use an opinion chart to write your ideas. When you are finished, put a star next to the idea you want to write about. Then put your completed list in your opinion text portfolio.*

Build Language Review: Verb Tense

Remind students that verbs are words that tell about actions, or what happens. Also remind them that present tense verbs, such as **look** and **walk**, tell about actions that are happening now.

- Point out that sometimes a present tense verb ends with an **s**.
- Display the following sentences and point out the verbs, eliciting help from volunteers.

> I **look** at the moon at night.
> John **protects** his eyes from the sun.
> She **gazes** at the stars.
> The children **count** the stars in the sky.

Present Tense Verbs Chart

Oral Language Practice

Invite partners to change the sentences in the previous activity by replacing the verb with another present-tense verb. For example: *I stare at the moon at night. John covers his eyes from the sun.*

(iELD) Integrated ELD

Light Support

Review present tense verbs.

Say: *Some present tense verbs end in the letter **s**.*
Display this chart:

In the Past	Right Now (Present)
traveled	
rotated	
moved	

Ask students to write the present tense verbs on the chart and act them out.

Moderate Support

Review present tense verbs.

Say: *Some present tense verbs end in the letter **s**.*
Write a list of present and past tense verbs on a chart. Ask students to identify present tense verbs and then act them out.

> rotates looks moves
> travels sat jumped
> sang waved walks

Substantial Support

Review present tense verbs.

Say: *Some present tense verbs end in the letter **s**.*
Write present tense verbs on cards, placing them facedown. Ask a student to pick a card and act it out. Have other students guess the verb.

Sample cards: **rotates, moves, walks, travels,** and **looks.**

W.1.1 Write opinion pieces in which they introduce the topic or name the book they are writing about, state an opinion, supply a reason for the opinion, and provide some sense of closure. **SL.1.1** Participate in collaborative conversations with diverse partners about grade 1 topics and texts with peers and adults in small and larger groups. **L.1.1e** Use verbs to convey a sense of past, present, and future (e.g., Yesterday I walked home; Today I walk home; Tomorrow I will walk home).

Student Objectives

I will be able to:
- List reasons for my opinion text.
- Use correct verb tenses for past and present.

Additional Materials

- Writing portfolios

Presentation BLMs 44 and 45
- Opinion Chart
- Verb Tense Chart

Opinion Text: Planning (10 MIN.) W.1.1, SL.1.1, L.1.1e

Engage Thinking

Review the Opinion Text Anchor Chart you created on Day 1 and point out that one feature is "states at least one reason for the opinion." Then display the Opinion chart you created on Day 2.

Say: *Yesterday, we brainstormed and chose a topic to write an opinion about. Then we put a star beside the topic we chose. Now we will plan our writing by listing reasons for the opinion we chose.*

Model

Pointing to the star on your Opinion chart, remind students that you chose to write an opinion about stars. Add a "Reason" column to the chart.

Sample think-aloud: *Now I will lists the reason or reasons for my opinion. When I think about why stars are interesting to look at, I like how they can form pictures in the sky. Long ago people named the pictures they saw. I'll add that reason to my chart. I also like the way stars sparkle at night. I'll add that reason to my chart as well.*

Topic	Opinion	Reason
Stars*	Stars are interesting to look at.	They form pictures in the night sky. Long ago, people named the giant pictures they saw.
		Stars sparkle in the night.

Sample Opinion Chart

Practice

Have partners share the reasons for their opinion about their chosen topic. Remind students to refer to their opinion chart.

Say: *Now you will do a quick write. You will have five minutes to draw or write a list of reasons to support your opinion. When you are finished, write your reasons on your opinion chart. Then put your completed Opinion chart in your opinion text portfolio.*

Build Language Review: Verb Tense

Remind students that verbs are words that tell about actions, or what happens. Explain that past tense verbs, such as **looked** and **walked,** tell about actions that have already happened. Point out that past tense verbs often end in **-ed.**

- Display the following sentences in both present and past tense.
- Ask students to identify each verb.
- Then guide students to identify context clues that help them determine the tense of each verb.

Present Tense Verbs	Past Tense Verbs
I look at the moon at night.	I looked at the moon last night.
John protects his eyes from the sun.	John protected his eyes from the sun yesterday.
We count the stars in the sky.	We counted the stars in the sky last night.

Verb Tense Chart

Oral Language Practice

Ask partners to turn to the inside back cover of *Night and Day* and generate sentences with past tense verbs. Have them look at the photos and captions for ideas as they describe the actions in the photos using past tense verbs. For example: *Astronomers used math to study objects in space. The satellites moved around Earth.*

iELD Integrated ELD

Light Support
Ask students to read their opinions from their charts. Then ask them, "Why do you think this?" Ask them to give a fact, detail, or example to explain their opinion. Then have them write their reason(s) in the chart.

Moderate Support
Review each column in the opinion chart with students, pointing out that the topic is the big idea, the opinion is something they think about the topic, and the reason supports their opinion.
Ask: *If you were asked why you like or don't like something, what would you say?*
Guide students to use language support such as: *I think ___ because ___.*

Substantial Support
Review each column in the Opinion chart with students, explaining that the topic is the big idea, the opinion is something they think about the topic, and the reason supports their opinion. Have students echo-read their opinions. Then ask students to act out their opinions and why they feel/think as they do. Guide them to dictate a sentence to explain their reasons. You might provide a sentence frame, such as: *I think ___ because ___.*

W.1.1 Write opinion pieces in which they introduce the topic or name the book they are writing about, state an opinion, supply a reason for the opinion, and provide some sense of closure. **SL.1.1** Participate in collaborative conversations with diverse partners about grade 1 topics and texts with peers and adults in small and larger groups. **L.1.1e** Use verbs to convey a sense of past, present, and future (e.g., Yesterday I walked home; Today I walk home; Tomorrow I will walk home).

Opinion Text: Draft Opinion and Reasons (10 MIN.) W.1.1, W.1.5, SL.1.1a, L.1.1e

Engage Thinking

Review the main features of an opinion text: naming a topic, stating an opinion, and providing reasons by referring to the anchor chart. Display and read the Opinion chart with students.

Say: *Planning gets us ready to begin writing. Now we'll use our opinion charts to write a draft of our opinion text.*

Model

Work with students to write an opinion text draft. Point out that they have chosen a topic that they have an opinion about and listed reasons to support their opinion. As you write each sentence, model how you apply your knowledge of print concepts, phonics, high-frequency words, and English language conventions.

> We can see stars in the night sky. Stars are interesting to look at. They form pictures in the night sky. Long ago, people named the giant pictures they saw. Stars sparkle in the night.

Sample Opinion Text Draft

Practice

Say: *Now turn to a partner and talk about the descriptive details and words you will add to your writing.*

Independent Writing

Say: *Now it's your turn to write an opinion text. Use the information in your opinion chart to name your topic, state your opinion, and provide reasons.*

Students may write during writer's workshop time or at a writing station during small-group reading time. Independent Writing should occur before the Partner Share. Use the Build Language Review as needed while you confer and monitor.

Additional Materials
• Writing portfolios

 Confer and Monitor

As students write independently, support their efforts as needed using prompts like those provided here.

Directive Feedback: *Look at your opinion chart to make sure you include the main elements of an opinion text.*

Self-Monitoring and Reflection: *Show me where you can add more reasons to support your opinion.*

Validating and Confirming: *I really like how you introduced your topic and stated your opinion.*

Partner Share

Say: *Now let's share our drafts with the group. Remember our three feedback skills: giving compliments, asking questions, and making suggestions? Pick one of those skills to practice now.*

Select a student as your partner and tell the class that you are going to practice giving a suggestion. Have your partner read his or her draft aloud. Then provide a suggestion that is positive, specific, and focused on improving your partner's draft. Then switch roles and model giving suggestions again.

Monitor partners as they share their drafts and provide feedback. Tell students to put their drafts in their opinion text portfolios.

Build Language Review: Verb Tense

Remind students that a verb tells about an action and a past tense verb tells about an action that has already happened. Also remind them that most past tense verbs end with **-ed.**

- Display examples of present tense verbs, such as: **move, look, turn.**
- Have students tell how to form the past tense of each verb you display.
- Write the past tense verbs on the board.

Oral Language Practice

Invite partners to take turns generating oral sentences using the past tense verbs from the Build Language activity. Challenge them to include an additional past tense verb in their sentences. For example: *Keiko moved fast down the hall! I looked both ways before I crossed the street.*

---

iELD Integrated ELD

Light Support
Review past tense verbs.
Say: *Past tense verbs often end in* **ed.**
Display this chart:

In the Past	Right Now (Present)
	travel
	rotate
	move

Ask students to write the past tense verbs on the chart and act them out.

Moderate Support
Review past tense verbs.
Say: *Past tense verbs often end in* **ed.**
Display a list of present and past tense verbs. Ask students to identify the past tense verbs and then act them out.

rotates	looked	moves
travels	painted	jumped
cooked	waved	walks

Substantial Support
Say: *Past tense verbs tell about something that happened in the past.*
Write past tense verbs on cards, placing them facedown. Ask a student to pick a card and act it out. Have other students guess the verb by saying, "Yesterday I _____."
Sample cards: **looked, read, clapped, jumped,** and **counted.**

W.1.1 Write opinion pieces in which they introduce the topic or name the book they are writing about, state an opinion, supply a reason for the opinion, and provide some sense of closure. **W.1.5** With guidance and support from adults, focus on a topic, respond to questions and suggestions from peers, and add details to strengthen writing as needed. **SL.1.1a** Follow agreed-upon rules for discussions (e.g., listening to others with care, speaking one at a time about the topics and texts under discussion). **L.1.1e** Use verbs to convey a sense of past, present, and future (e.g., Yesterday I walked home; Today I walk home; Tomorrow I will walk home).

Opinion Text: Draft a Conclusion and Title (10 MIN.) W.1.1, W.1.5, SL.1.6, L.1.1e

Engage Thinking

Review the main elements of an opinion text on the Anchor Chart.

Say: *Yesterday, you wrote your first draft of an opinion text. Your draft has a topic, opinion, and reasons. An opinion text also needs a conclusion, or ending. A conclusion restates the opinion and provides a strong ending to their writing. Today you will write a conclusion and add a title to your opinion text.*

Model

Work with students to develop their drafts. Model adding a title and strong ending that restates the opinion. As you write each sentence, model how you apply your knowledge of print concepts, phonics, high-frequency words, and English language conventions.

Sky Watching

by _____

We can see stars in the night sky. Stars are interesting to look at. They form pictures in the night sky. Long ago, people named the giant pictures they saw. Stars sparkle in the night. The more we look at the stars, the more we can learn about the stars that light the sky at night.

Sample Opinion Text Draft

Practice

Invite partners to read their drafts out loud and look at it together. Have students discuss titles and closing sentences with their partners. Suggest that students look back at their topics to help them write a title. To help them write a strong ending, tell them to summarize their topic by restating their opinion.

Independent Writing

Say: *Now it's your turn to work on your draft. Add a title that tells what your opinion text is about. Think about one last idea you want to share about your topic. Write a conclusion to share this idea.*

Students may write during writer's workshop time or at a writing station during small-group reading time. Independent Writing should occur before the Whole-Group Share. Use the Build Language Review as needed while you confer and monitor.

Student Objectives

I will be able to:
• Write a strong ending for my opinion text.
• Use correct present verb tenses.

Additional Materials

• Writing portfolios

 **Confer and Monitor**

As students write independently, support their efforts as needed using prompts like those provided here.

Directive Feedback: *Use the following sentence frame to help you draft a conclusion for your opinion text:* I think _____.

Self-Monitoring and Reflection: *Read your draft again. What is your topic? Use your topic name in your title.*

Validating and Confirming: *Your title states what your opinion text is about, and your conclusion helps readers understand your opinion.*

Whole-Group Share

Say: *Now let's share our writing with the group. First, read the title of your opinion text. Then read your text out loud.*

Assist as needed as students share their writing with the group. Remind students to put their drafts in the opinion text portfolios.

Build Language Review: Verb Tense

Review with students that verbs are words that tell about actions. Elicit from students that present tense verbs tell about actions that are happening now.

- Display examples of past tense verbs, such as **changed, appeared,** and **traveled.**
- Point out that these verbs all tell about the past and you need help changing them to tell about the present.
- Have volunteers change the tense of each verb from past to present.
- Write the present tense verbs on the board.

Oral Language Practice

Have partners take turns generating oral sentences to share their opinions about the text *Night and Day*. Ask them to use present tense verbs in their sentences. For example: *My favorite part is when I learn the moon changes shape each night.*

 **Integrated ELD**

Light Support
Guide students to think of an idea to add a conclusion to their opinion texts. For example, have them think about something they want to do to see their favorite thing in the sky. Remind them to use complete sentences in their oral responses.

Moderate Support
Guide students to think of an idea to add a conclusion to their opinion texts. For example, provide partners with a sentence frame to tell something they want to do in order to see their favorite thing in the sky. Have partners respond orally.
I want to ___ to see ___ in the sky.

Substantial Support
Explain to students that one way to end their opinion texts about favorite things in the sky is to tell about something they like to do or want to go see.
With students, complete the sentence frames orally and in writing. Have students echo-read:
I want to ___ to see ___ in the sky.

W.1.1 Write opinion pieces in which they introduce the topic or name the book they are writing about, state an opinion, supply a reason for the opinion, and provide some sense of closure., **W.1.5** With guidance and support from adults, focus on a topic, respond to questions and suggestions from peers, and add details to strengthen writing as needed. **SL.1.6** Produce complete sentences when appropriate to task and situation. **L.1.1e** Use verbs to convey a sense of past, present, and future (e.g., Yesterday I walked home; Today I walk home; Tomorrow I will walk home).

Opinion Text: Use Linking Words

(10 MIN.) W.1.1, L.1.1e

Engage Thinking

Remind students that strong writers revise and add words to their drafts to make their writing better.

Say: *We wrote our drafts. Now we will revise our opinion texts by adding linking works to make our writing stronger. The word **because** is a linking word and can be used to show how an opinion connects to a reason.*

Model

Work with students to revise an opinion text draft. Show them how to incorporate linking words such as **because** to describe how an opinion is clearly connected to the reason that supports the opinion. As you write each sentence, model how you apply your knowledge of prints concepts, phonics, high-frequency words, and English language conventions.

Sky Watching

by _____

We can see stars in the night sky. Stars are interesting to look at. One reason stars are interesting is because they form pictures in the night sky. Long ago people named the giant pictures they saw. I also enjoy watching the stars sparkle at night. The more we look at the stars, the more we can learn about the stars that light the sky at night.

Sample Opinion Text Draft

Practice

Have students read their opinion text drafts with their partners. Working together, students should identify points in their drafts where linking words would make their writing stronger. Display linking words, such as **because, and, also.**

Independent Writing

Provide time for students to write individually.

Students may write during writer's workshop time or at a writing station during small-group reading time. Independent Writing should occur before the Partner Share. Use the Build Language Review as needed while you confer and monitor.

 **Confer and Monitor**

As students revise independently, support their efforts as needed using prompts like those provided here.

Directive Feedback: *Look at your draft and find the parts where you support your opinion with reasons. Think of some linking words you can add to connect the reasons to your opinion.*

Self-Monitoring and Reflection: *When you explain your reasons for your opinion, do you use linking words?*

Validating and Confirming: *I like how you used linking words to connect your ideas and made the beginning of your sentences stronger.*

Partner Share

Say: *Now share your writing with a partner. Read your opinion texts to each other. Point out where you've added words that connect your opinion to support the reasons.*

Monitor partners as they share their writing. Remind them to put their revised drafts in their Opinion Text portfolios.

Build Language Review: Verb Tense (iELD)

Say: *Remember that we use different verbs for telling about things that happen in the past, present, and future. A past tense verb tells about something that has already happened.*

- Use examples to tell about things that have recently happened in the classroom or at the school. For example:

> We **counted** to 20 yesterday.
> We **learned** about night and day last week.
> The cafeteria **served** tacos on Tuesday.

- Have students explain how each verb is past tense.
- As time allows, brainstorm with students or have volunteers suggest other past tense verbs that may not end in **-ed.**

Oral Language Practice

Invite pairs of students to take turns generating oral sentences that use past tense verbs. Encourage them to tell about details from the text *The Wind and the Sun.*

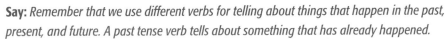

(iELD) Integrated ELD

Light Support
Say: *Not all past tense verbs end in* **-ed.** *Some change form.*
Display this chart:

In the Past	Right Now (Present)
	eat
	fall
	run
	sit
	write

Ask students to write the past tense verbs on the chart and act them out.

Moderate Support
Review past tense verbs.
Say: *Not all past tense verbs end in* **-ed.** *Some change form.*
Display this chart:

In the Past	Right Now (Present)
	eat
	fall
	run

Ask students to write the past tense verbs on the chart and act them out.

Substantial Support
Review past tense verbs.
Say: *Past tense verbs end in* **-ed.**

Past	Present

Write present and past tense verbs on self-stick notes. Ask a student to pick a verb and place it on the correct column on the chart.
Sample verbs: *smiled, run, sip, clapped, jumped, cry, counted,* and *fly.*

W.1.1 Write opinion pieces in which they introduce the topic or name the book they are writing about, state an opinion, supply a reason for the opinion, and provide some sense of closure. **L.1.1e** Use verbs to convey a sense of past, present, and future (e.g., Yesterday I walked home; Today I walk home; Tomorrow I will walk home).

© Benchmark Education Company, LLC

Grade 1 • Unit 8 • Week 3   **93**

Opinion Text: Revise to Add Another Reason (10 MIN.) W.1.1, W.1.5, L.1.1e

Student Objectives

I will be able to:
• Revise my opinion text.
• Add another reason to support my opinion text.
• Use correct past tense verbs.

Additional Materials

• Writing portfolios

Engage Thinking

Display the Opinion Text draft. Remind students that yesterday you began to revise your opinion texts.

Say: *When writers revise, they improve their writing by adding or taking away words, phrases, or sentences. Today we will revise our drafts by adding another reason to support our opinion.*

Model

Work with students to revise an opinion text draft. Explain that adding another reason to their writing will help support their opinion and make their opinion text stronger. As you write each sentence, model how you apply your knowledge of print concepts, phonics, high-frequency words, and English language conventions.

> **Sky Watching**
> **by** _____
>
> We can see stars in the night sky. Stars are interesting to look at. One reason stars are interesting is because they form pictures in the night sky. Long ago people named the giant pictures they saw. I also enjoy watching the stars sparkle at night. As I look up at the sky, I notice large and smaller stars in different colors. The more we look at the stars, the more we can learn about the stars that light the night sky.

Sample Opinion Text Draft

Practice

Have students work with their partners and read their own opinion text drafts. Students should help their partners look for places where stating another reason to support their opinion can improve their text.

Independent Writing (iELD)

Provide time for students to write individually.

Students may write during writer's workshop time or at a writing station during small-group reading time. Independent Writing should occur before the Partner Share. Use the Build Language Review as needed while you confer and monitor.

 **Confer and Monitor**

As students revise independently, support their efforts as needed using prompts like those provided here.

Directive Feedback: *Look at your draft and identify the reason you wrote for your opinion. Think of another reason that supports your opinion.*

Self-Monitoring and Reflection: *How can adding another reason to support your opinion make your writing better?*

Validating and Confirming: *The reason you added really supports your opinion and makes your opinion text stronger.*

Partner Share

Say: *Now let's share our drafts with partners. Read your draft out loud. Point out the reason you added to your opinion text.*

Monitor partners as they share their writing. Remind students to put their drafts in their Opinion Text portfolios.

Build Language Review: Verb Tense

Say: *Remember that we use different verbs for telling about things that happen in the past, present, and future. A past tense verb tells about something that has already happened.*

- Point out that most past tense verbs end with **-ed** but that some are irregular, such as **blew** and **shone.**
- Display example sentences and point out each verb to students.
- Then ask volunteers to identify the present tense of each regular or irregular verb.

Past Tense Verbs
Wind and Sun **competed** in a contest.
Wind **blew** harder and harder.
Sun **shone** on the traveler.
The traveler **removed** his cloak.

Past Tense Verbs Chart

Oral Language Practice

Ask partners to tell more about the story of *The Wind and the Sun* by filling in key details missing from the summary used in Build Language. Remind them to use past tense verbs in their oral sentences to retell or summarize what happens in the story. For example: *Wind thought he was stronger than Sun. Wind wanted to go first.*

iELD Integrated ELD

Light Support
Review student drafts of their opinion text. Ask students to say at least two oral sentences explaining their reasons for their opinion. Then have students practice writing at least one of the reasons they might add to their drafts. Have students read their answers to the group.

Moderate Support
Review student drafts of their opinion text. Remind students they can give more than one reason or example supporting their opinion.
Say: *I like _____ because _____.*
Ask partners to fill in the sentence frame, choosing one more example and citing a reason for their opinion. Have partners read their answers to the group.

Substantial Support
Review student drafts of their opinion text.
Say: *What are some reasons that is your favorite thing in the sky? Tell me why you feel that way.*
Remind students to give a reason for their opinion.
Say: *I like _____ because _____.*
As a group, fill in the sentence frame choosing one example and citing the reason.

W.1.1 Write opinion pieces in which they introduce the topic or name the book they are writing about, state an opinion, supply a reason for the opinion, and provide some sense of closure. **W.1.5** With guidance and support from adults, focus on a topic, respond to questions and suggestions from peers, and add details to strengthen writing as needed., **L.1.1e** Use verbs to convey a sense of past, present, and future (e.g., Yesterday I walked home; Today I walk home; Tomorrow I will walk home).

Opinion Text: Edit for End Punctuation (10 MIN.) W.1.1, L.1.1d, L.1.2b

Engage Thinking

Display your opinion text draft from Day 2. Remind students that this is your revised draft.

Say: *Now that we have finished revising, we will look closely at our drafts to fix any mistakes. When we fix mistakes in our writing, we are editing. Today I'm going to edit my draft by checking my end punctuation.*

Model

First, display your revisions, and discuss the changes you made and why you made them.

- *You added words to the beginning of the fifth sentence to ask a question. Then you changed the period to a question mark at the end of the sentence.*
- *You changed the period to an exclamation point at the end of the last sentence to show excitement.*

Sample Opinion Text Draft

Practice

Ask students to read their final draft to their partner and identify some edits they might make to strengthen their text. Tell students that working with partners helps with editing. A reader can often catch mistakes the writer cannot see. Students should find at least one end punctuation mark to change in their drafts.

Independent Writing

Provide time for students to write individually.

Students may draw and write during writer's workshop time or at a writing station during small-group reading time. Independent Writing should occur before the Partner Share and Build Language Review activities.

Student Objectives

I will be able to:
- Edit my opinion text.
- Use correct end punctuation.
- Use correct present tense verbs.

Additional Materials

- Writing portfolios
Presentation BLM 46
- Pronoun Chart

Confer and Monitor

As students edit independently, support their efforts as needed using prompts like those provided here.

Directive Feedback: *Make sure to check your spelling, capitalization, and use of end punctuation marks in your drafts.*

Self-Monitoring and Reflection: *Think of the other writing pieces you have edited. What things do you find yourself fixing? Look for those issues in your story.*

Validating and Confirming: *You did a careful job editing and finding the mistakes with end punctuation in your writing.*

Partner Share

Say: *Now let's share our edited drafts with partners. Read your draft out loud. Point out what changes you made and why you made each change.*

Monitor partners as they share their writing. Remind students to put their edited draft in their Opinion Text portfolio.

Build Language Review: Use Pronouns

Say: *Remember that a pronoun takes the place of a noun. Personal pronouns include **I**, **you**, and **we**. Possessive pronouns include **my** and **our**. Examples of indefinite pronouns include **anybody** and **everybody**.*

Display the following sentences and ask volunteers to identify each type of pronoun used.

Sentence	Type of Pronoun
We can see stars in the night sky.	[personal]
One reason stars are interesting is because **they** form pictures.	[personal]
Karla looked through **her** telescope.	[possessive]
She saw **something** race through the night sky.	[personal, indefinite]

Pronoun Chart

Oral Language Practice
Ask student pairs to look at the sentences in the Build Language activity. Partners take turns replacing the pronouns with proper or common nouns. For example: *Sarah saw a comet race through the night sky.*

(iELD) Integrated ELD

Light Support
Display this chart. Review periods, question marks, and exclamation points. Ask students to place the correct punctuation mark at the end of each sentence. Call on volunteers to share their answers. Discuss situations where multiple correct answers are possible.

"Look at me"	
He will leave town tomorrow	
He tore off his cloak	
The wind gave up	
Who will win the contest	

Moderate Support
Review periods, question marks, and exclamation points. Give students cards with one of the three ending marks on each.
Say: *Hold up the card with the correct ending mark.*

"Look at me"	
Do you see a traveler	
He tore off his cloak	
Can you melt the ice cream	
Who will win the contest	

Substantial Support
Review periods and question marks. Give each student a card with a question mark and one with a period.
Ask: *Question or statement? Hold up the card with the correct ending mark.*

The wind blew harder still	
Do you see a traveler	
He tore off his cloak	
Can you melt the ice cream	

W.1.1 Write opinion pieces in which they introduce the topic or name the book they are writing about, state an opinion, supply a reason for the opinion, and provide some sense of closure. **L.1.1d** Use personal, possessive, and indefinite pronouns (e.g., I, me, my; they, them, their, anyone, everything). **L.1.2b** Use end punctuation for sentences.

Publish the Opinion Text (10 MIN.) W.1.1, W.1.6, L.1.1d

Engage Thinking

Remind students that in the last two weeks, you have been working together to write opinion texts. Display and reread your mentor text. When you finish, spend a few moments reviewing the processes you went through to plan, draft, revise, and edit your opinion text.

Sky Watching
by _____

We can see stars in the night sky. Stars are interesting to look at. One reason stars are interesting is because they form pictures in the night sky. Did you know that long ago people named the giant pictures they saw? I also enjoy watching the stars sparkle at night. As I look up at the sky, I notice large and smaller stars in different colors. The more we look at the stars, the more we can learn about the stars that light the night sky!

Opinion Mentor Text

Say: *Today we will publish our opinion text. I published my opinion text by typing it on a word processing program on a computer. You can also publish your opinion text by writing a neat, final copy.*

Create a Publishing Checklist

You may create a new publishing checklist or adapt the list you created for Unit 6.

Ask: *What our published opinion texts should include.*

Feature	Digital Publication	Handwritten
title at top	X	X
author's name under title	X	X
darker font for title and author	X	
clear handwriting		X
correct spacing	X	X
add a drawing (optional)	X	X

Publishing Checklist

Peer Collaboration (IELD)

Have students read their final drafts aloud to a partner and decide how they're going to publish their opinion texts.

Publication

Students may publish during writer's workshop time or at a writing station during small-group reading time. Remind students to put their published pieces in their Opinion Text portfolios.

Build Language Review: Use Pronouns

Remind students that a pronoun replaces a proper or common noun.

- Ask students to use pronouns to tell about things that are happening in the classroom or on the playground that day. For example: *We are working on our writing.*
- You may wish to provide a variety of subjects for students to use so they will generate sentences with multiple kinds of pronouns.

Oral Language Practice

Invite partners to take turns generating oral sentences by sharing opinions about the text *The Wind and the Sun.* Ask them to share opinions using pronouns. For example: *I think it is silly that Wind thinks he is stronger than Sun.*

(iELD) Integrated ELD

Light Support
Have students publish their opinion text. Give students a checklist for publishing and a template they can use to write their final copies. Have them keep the fully executed check list in their portfolios.

Moderate Support
Have students publish their opinion text. Give students a checklist for publishing and a template for writing that has labels for each piece of the text, such as *name, title, picture,* and *text.* Have them keep the fully executed check list in their portfolios.

Substantial Support
Have students publish their opinion text. Give students a template for writing that has labels for each piece of the text, such as *name, title, picture,* and *text.* Give students a model to follow that shows how to use the template. Have them keep the fully executed checklist in their portfolios.

W.1.1 Write opinion pieces in which they introduce the topic or name the book they are writing about, state an opinion, supply a reason for the opinion, and provide some sense of closure. **W.1.6** With guidance and support from adults, use a variety of digital tools to produce and publish writing, including in collaboration with peers. **L.1.1d** Use personal, possessive, and indefinite pronouns (e.g., I, me, my; they, them, their, anyone, everything)..

Share Opinion Texts (10 MIN.) W.1.1

Engage Thinking

Display and read the published copy of your opinion text.

> **Sky Watching**
> **by** _____
>
> We can see stars in the night sky. Stars are interesting to look at. One reason stars are interesting is because they form pictures in the night sky. Did you know that long ago people named the giant pictures they saw? I also enjoy watching the stars sparkle at night. As I look up at the sky, I notice large and smaller stars in different colors. The more we look at the stars, the more we can learn about the stars that light the night sky!

Opinion Mentor Text

Say: _During the past two weeks, we have learned many steps writers take when they work. We brainstormed ideas. We planned our writing. We drafted, revised, and edited our work. Finally, we published our writing. Now we are ready to share our published writing with others. Now we're going to practice giving a compliment, asking a question, and offering a suggestion to a partner on their opinion text._

Model Peer Collaboration

Read aloud your published opinion text. Then ask a volunteer to introduce their opinion text and read it aloud. After reading, model how you give the writer a compliment using a sentence frame such as:

- _I like how you _____ because it helped me _____._
- _My favorite part was _____ because _____._
- _It was really interesting when _____ and I liked that because _____._

Remind students that compliments can be about any part of the work, but they should always describe something positive and point to something specific in the writer's work. Point out that your compliment is kind and specific.

Allow partners to read their opinion text and give each other compliments.

Next, model asking questions. Return to your student-partner's opinion text and model asking questions with sentence frames such as:

- _When we were brainstorming topics, how did you decide on _____ (topic)?_

Student Objectives

I will be able to:
- Share my opinion text with a partner.
- Compliment, question, and make suggestions on a partner's opinion text.

Additional Materials

- Writing portfolios

- *What revision do you think made the biggest difference to your writing?*
- *What was the hardest part of your writing?*
- *What is your favorite part of your opinion text?*

Point out that questions can be about the details of the writers' work or about the how the writer created their opinion text. Either way, the questions should be friendly and focus on an important aspect of writing.

Allow students time to ask their partner questions.

Finally, model offering a suggestion. Return to your student-partner's opinion text and model offering your partner a suggestion to improve their writing. Use the following samples to help craft your own suggestion.

- Adding a picture of the writer star-watching would help the reader understand the writer's feelings and opinion.
- It would be interesting to learn the names people gave the stars that make giant pictures in the sky.
- *I would love to know which is your favorite place to watch the stars.*

Explain to students that suggestions must be kind, specific to the text, and helpful to the writer. Review your own modeled suggestion and point out how it meets this criteria.

Allow time for students to review their partner's work and offer suggestions.

Practice Peer Collaboration

Invite partners to read their published opinion texts out loud and give compliments, ask questions, and make suggestions about each other's work.

Whole-Group Share

Select a few students to share their opinion texts with the whole group. Invite class members to give compliments, ask questions, and make suggestions about each student's work.

Place the opinion texts in your classroom library for students to reread throughout the rest of the school year. Alternatively, allow students to take their portfolios home and/or file them to use as documentation of students' developing writing skills.

(iELD) Integrated ELD

Light Support
Ask student pairs to practice making suggestions using the Mentor Text before sharing their own writing. Have them pretend that their partner wrote the Opinion Mentor Text and think about at least one way they could add to the opinion text.

Moderate Support
Ask student pairs to practice asking questions using the Mentor Text before sharing their own writing. Have them echo-read the Mentor Text first. Then have them think about any questions they want to ask about the text, pretending their partner is the writer. Encourage them to use sentence frames:
Why did you ___?
Why do you think ___?

Substantial Support
Have students echo-read the Mentor Text. Then guide students to practice giving compliments using the Mentor Text before sharing their own writing. You might encourage them to use a sentence frame:
I like ___.

W.1.1 Write opinion pieces in which they introduce the topic or name the book they are writing about, state an opinion, supply a reason for the opinion, and provide some sense of closure.

Informational Report: Analyze a Prompt and Read a Mentor Text (10 MIN.)

W.1.2, L.1.1f

Engage Thinking

Explain that, over the next to weeks, you will work together to write a informational report.

Say: *An informational report is a nonfiction writing that includes facts about a topic. We will start the writing process by reading a prompt. The prompt tells us what we will write about. The prompt also helps us plan our writing by telling us what we must include in our work.*

Analyze the Prompt

Display and distribute copies of the writing prompt. Read aloud the prompt, then use a think-aloud to model how you analyze it.

Sample think-aloud: *This prompt starts with a question: "What important good or service do you use every day?" I am supposed to answer that question. I see the word **or** and I know that I am supposed to pick one good or one service to describe. What else does the prompt tell me?*

Work with students to analyze the rest of the prompt. Guide students to identify the following key requirements included in the prompt:

- The answer should include an explanation of why the good or service is important.
- The answer must be supported with facts and definitions.
- The student must use *In My Opinion… Goods and Services Are Important* and *We Use Goods and Services* as resources.

Read the Mentor Text

Introduce the mentor text as a model. Tell students to listen closely for all the requirements specified in the prompt.

> **I Love My Computer!**
> **By** _____
> My computer is an important good that I use every day. A good is something that is made or grown and sold and bought. My laptop computer was built by a technology company. I bought it at the electronics store. Goods are also things that people need and want. I need my computer at work and at home. My computer helps me at work. I use it to e-mail my coworkers and plan my daily lessons. My computer helps me at home. I use my computer to keep up with my family on social media and buy things I need. Finally, my computer is fun. I watch movies, television, and videos on my computer. Every day, I use my computer to make my work easier and my free time more interesting!

Informational Report Mentor Text

Student Writing Prompt

What important good or service do you use every day? Explain why this good or service is important to you. Support your ideas with facts and definitions from the book *In My Opinion . . . Goods and Services Are Important* and the video *We Use Goods and Services*.

Student Objectives

I will be able to:
- Use an informational text planning guide.
- Draft an introduction to a topic for an informational text.

Additional Materials

- Writing portfolio
Presentation BLM 48
- Adjectives Chart

Analyze the Mentor Text

Say: *Let's use this text to analyze the parts, or features, of my informational report.*

As you go through the text, point out the following features and list them on a chart:

> A informational report has:
> • a title and author
> • an introduction with a main idea
> • an explanation of the main idea
> • supporting facts and definitions
> • a closing sentence about the main idea

Informational Text Anchor Chart

Quick Write

Say: *Now let's do a quick write as a warm-up. Take five minutes and write about services or goods that you've used today. What did you use and why?*

Explain that this activity will help students prepare for writing the longer informational report they will write later this week. When students finish, tell them to add their quick writes to their Informational Text portfolios.

Build Language: Adjectives (iELD) (10 MIN.) L.1.1f

Tell students that an adjective is a word that describes a person, place, or thing. Explain that adjectives help describe nouns. Display the chart below. Read the sentence aloud. Then read the question in the second column. Work with students to add an adjective that revises the sentence to answer the question.

Original Sentence	Question	New Sentence with an Adjective
Bill lives in a house.	What kind of house?	Bill lives in a huge house.
We bought coats.	What kind of coats?	
The car was parked by the curb.	What kind of car?	
The garden was full of flowers.	What kind of flowers?	

Oral Language Practice

Have partners continue the activity by taking turns saying sentences with nouns and asking a question about the noun in their sentence. The student's partner should then respond with a revised sentence that includes an adjective and answers the question. For example: *We told a story. What kind of story. We told a scary story.*

iELD) Integrated ELD

Light Support
Display pages 4 and 5 of the book *Goods and Services Are Important.* Have partners look at the photographs and create descriptive sentences for items they see. Tell the students to use adjectives in their sentences. For example: *The lady is wearing a red shirt. The farmer is holding green ears of corn.*

Moderate Support
Display pages 4 and 5 of the book *Goods and Services Are Important.* Point to objects in the photographs and ask the group for adjectives that describe them. When a student offers a particularly strong or interesting adjective, work with the group to create a descriptive sentence that properly uses the adjective to describe the object in the photograph.

Substantial Support
Display pages 4 and 5 of the book *Goods and Services Are Important.* Write the following sentences for the students to see.
• The happy farmer has a hat.
• The smiling woman is shopping.
• The lemonade stand has a brown and yellow sign.
Work with the students to find these objects in the photographs. Point out to students the adjective in each sentence and show the connection to the photographs. Select other objects from the photographs and ask the students to volunteer to provide adjectives that describe them.

W.1.2 Write informative/explanatory texts in which they name a topic, supply some facts about the topic, and provide some sense of closure. **L.1.1f** Use frequently occurring adjectives.

Informational Report: Brainstorm

(10 MIN.) W.1.2, W.1.7, SL.1.5, L.1.1f

Engage Thinking

Display the Informational Text Anchor Chart you created on Day 1.

Say: *Now we will brainstorm topics for our informational report. While we brainstorm, let's keep the anchor chart in mind. We want to think of topics that help us create all the things we know a strong informational report must have.*

Model

Use a think-aloud to model generating a list of possible informational report topics. Encourage students to focus on topics they like and know well. Remind them of the Day 1 Quick Write, when they wrote about services and goods that they use.

Sample think-aloud: *The prompt gave me a specific focus for my informational report. I will brainstorm goods and services that I use every day and that are very important to me.*

Create a topic list. For example:

> **Topic Ideas**
> 1. My car - how I get to work
> 2. My computer - helps me with work
> 3. Radio station broadcast - listen every day
> 4. School janitorial staff - always keeps my workplace clean

Sample think-aloud: *Now I'll look at the list I created. All of these are important services and goods I use every day. What topic is something I could support with facts and definitions. I think I'll pick my computer to write about.*

Practice (IELD)

Say: *Turn and talk to your partner about the topics you might want to write about. As you think of topics, explain to your partner why each good or service you think of is important. Share with your partner what topics you think will be the most challenging and why. Remember to listen to your partner as he or she shares ideas with you.*

 Quick Write

Say: *Now it's your turn to brainstorm ideas. You have five minutes to write a list of topics you could use for your informational report. When you finish, review your list and draw a star next to the topic you want to write about. Then put your completed list in your Informational Text portfolio.*

Build Language Review: Adjectives

Remind students that they have learned that adjectives are words that describe nouns. Explain that when they describe a person, place, or thing, they can ask themselves "What adjectives would help me describe it?" Next, select items around the room and ask the students to volunteer adjectives to describe them.

Ask: *What adjectives describe this desk?*

Have students put in the following sentence frame: *That is a _____ desk.*

Continue with other objects until students are ready to continue the pattern of item selection and response as partners.

Oral Language Practice

Have partners continue the Build Language activity. Each partner should take turns selecting items around the room and saying descriptive sentences that use adjectives.

 **Integrated ELD**

Light Support
Have students divide into groups and play Adjective 20 Questions. One student selects an object in the room. The student cannot select a person or a piece of clothing. Next, the other students in the group ask questions, using adjectives. For example: *Is it red? Is it flat?* After each question, the student asking the question can guess what the item is. If a student guesses correctly, he or she becomes the next selector. If no student has guessed in 20 questions, the first student shares what he or she selected and the role of selector passes on to another student in the group.

Moderate Support
Play as above, but take the role of the selector. Have the students work together to guess what you've selected. Remove the 20-question cap and assist them by helping them pick strong, useful adjectives.

Substantial Support
Select an adjective and write it where it is displayed for the student. Select a common adjective your students will easily recognize. Work with the students to define it. Next, work with the students to come up with three nouns that the adjective can describe.
For example: *Our adjective is **large**. **Large** means "big."*
1. elephant
2. building
3. mountain
Ask students to volunteer an adjective to repeat.

W.1.2 Write informative/explanatory texts in which they name a topic, supply some facts about the topic, and provide some sense of closure. **W.1.7** Participate in shared research and writing projects (e.g. explore a number of ""how-to"" books on a given topic and use them to write a sequence of instructions). **SL.1.5** Add drawings or other visual displays to descriptions when appropriate to clarify ideas, thoughts, and feelings. **L.1.1f** Use frequently occurring adjectives.

Informational Report: Find Details in Text Sources (10 MIN.) W.1.2, W.1.7, L.1.1f

Engage Thinking

Reread the writing prompt with students. Point out the sources indicated in the prompt. Tell students that today they will read and take notes from the printed source text.

Model

Remind students of the topic you chose to write about. Tell them that you are going to reread *In My Opinion… Goods and Services Are Important,* paying special attention to facts and details that will help describe the good or service you selected and that will help readers understand why this good or service is so important to you. Model pausing as you read to take notes. When you take notes, point out the language of the original text and model summarizing that language into a note for your own use. For example:

• *(On page 2.) It says here that a good is something that "people grow, make, buy, or sell." That's a very good definition of a good and describes my computer. Somebody made it and sold it. I bought it. I'll make a note of that.*

Continue through the process, adding at least two more facts or definitions to your notetaking chart.

Source: *Goods and Service Are Important*	**Notes**
Goods are things that people grow, make, buy, or sell. Food, clothing, cars, and homes are examples of goods.	Goods are things that are made, sold, and bought.
In my opinion, goods made for technology are important because they make people's lives easier.	Technology makes life easier.
Computers help people do their work and learn new skills.	Computers help people work.

Sample Notetaking Chart

Practice

Have students work in pairs and reread *Good and Services Are Important* to find facts and definitions they can use in their writing. Have partners remind each other of their topics. Have them review the text, find relevant details, and help each other summarize the wording of the source. Remind students that notes should be in their own words.

Quick Write

Say: *Now it's your turn to take notes for your writing. Find two or three facts and definitions that you can use in your writing. You have five minutes to write down you notes. We will be adding more notes later, so be sure to place your notes in your Informational Text portfolio when you are done.*

Build Language Review: Adjectives

Remind students that adjectives are words that describe people, places, and things. Brainstorm with the class examples of nouns and adjectives that students might use when drafting their informational text. List examples on a chart and keep the chart displayed for students to refer to as they do their writing. For example:

Nouns	Adjectives
food	tasty, healthy
farmers	hardworking, important
nurses	skillful, kind
computers	new, gray
airplanes	fast, high
teachers	great, interesting

Oral Language Practice

Have partners take turns choosing a noun and an adjective from the chart and saying a sentence that contains both.

Integrated ELD

Light Support

Review summarizing to help students take useful notes. Share the following notes with the group. Have partners circle the useful notes. For the notes they did not circle, partners should explain why the notes are not helpful.

Sample Notes:
Food is healthful.
Doctors and nurses
Teachers help students learn.
Explore and solve problems.

Have partners share their work with the class. Guide discussion to resolve errors and show students that helpful notes capture key details and ideas.

Moderate Support

Present the notes above. As a group, work together to evaluate each sample note. Determine whether each note is useful or not on the basis of whether or not it captures a complete detail or idea.

Substantial Support

Review summarizing by comparing a source text and a useful note that captures the important information from the source text.

Source Text: In my opinion, the most important good is food because people cannot live without it.

Note: People need food to live.

Show students how the note states the most important fact and records that fact in the notetakers' own words.

Work with students to write a note that summarizes the following sentence:

Source Text: Telephones , computers, and ways to travel help make people's lives easier.

W.1.2 Write informative/explanatory texts in which they name a topic, supply some facts about the topic, and provide some sense of closure. **W.1.7** Participate in shared research and writing projects (e.g. explore a number of "how-to" books on a given topic and use them to write a sequence of instructions). **L.1.1f** Use frequently occurring adjectives.

Informational Report: Find Facts in Media Sources (10 MIN.) W.1.2, W.1.7, L.1.1f

Engage Thinking

Remind students that they took notes on useful facts and definitions from *In My Opinion…Goods and Services Are Important.* Tell students that they will practice notetaking again, but this time they will be watching and listening to the video *We Use Goods and Services.*

Model

Remind students of the topic of your informational report. Tell them that you are going to play the video "We Use Good and Services," paying special attention to facts and details that will help describe the good or service you selected and that will help readers understand why this good or service is so important to you. Point out that you will be looking for details in the video's visuals and be listening for helpful details and definitions.

Play the video. Model pausing the video to take notes. When you take notes, point out the language or imagery of the original video. Show how you summarize the information in your own words. For example:

- *The video says that "People buy goods and services to get what they need and want." I can add that to the definition of goods I took from* Goods and Services Are Important. *My computer is definitely something I need and something I want. I'll make a note of that.*

Continue through the process. Adding additional facts or definitions to your notetaking chart as appropriate.

Source: *We Use Goods and Services*	**Notes**
People buy goods and services to get what they need and want.	A good is something you need or want.

Sample Notetaking Chart

Practice (iELD)

Replay the video. Have students turn to their partners and discuss facts and definitions from the video that they can use in their writing. Have them tell their partners about relevant details, and ask them to help each other summarize these facts and ideas for their notes. Remind students that notes should be in their own words.

Quick Write

Say: *Now it's your turn to take notes for your writing. Find two or three facts and definitions that you can use in your writing. You have five minutes to write down you notes. We will be using these notes later, so be sure to place your notes in your Informational Text portfolio when you are done.*

Build Language Review: Adjectives

Replay the video. Pause at the 0:07 mark, on the image of the family grocery shopping. Ask students to help you describe the scene using adjectives. Display the following chart. Have students describe each noun in a full sentence using at least one adjective. Record the adjectives in the chart. For example: *The father is tall. The father is wearing a blue, green, and white shirt.*

Noun	Adjectives
Father	tall, green, white, blue
Mother	
Children	
Food	

Adjective Chart

Oral Language Practice

Pause the video at the 0:15 mark, on the image of the students in the classroom. Have partners work in pairs to create descriptive sentences, as they did above, using at least one adjective in each sentence. Each partner should create one complete descriptive sentence.

(iELD) Integrated ELD

Light Support
Pause the video at 0:04-second mark, on the image of introductory collection of goods and services. Have students divide into groups and play Adjective 20 Questions. One student selects an object in the image from the video. The other students in the group ask questions, using adjectives. For example: *Is it blue? Is it sweet?* After each question, the student asking the question can guess what the item is. If a student guesses correctly, they become the next selector. If no student has guessed in 20 questions, the first student shares what they selected and the role of selector passes on to another student in the group.

Moderate Support
Play as above, but take the role of the selector. Have the students work together to guess what you've selected. Remove the 20-question cap and assist them by helping them pick strong, useful adjectives.

Substantial Support
Pause the video at 0:04-second mark, on the image of introductory collection of goods and services. For each image, work with the group to identify adjectives that describe the image. Start with the honey.
Say: *Honey is . . .*
1. sweet
2. gold
3. sticky

W.1.2 Write informative/explanatory texts in which they name a topic, supply some facts about the topic, and provide some sense of closure. **W.1.7** Participate in shared research and writing projects (e.g. explore a number of "how-to" books on a given topic and use them to write a sequence of instructions). **L.1.1f** Use frequently occurring adjectives.

Informational Report: Planning (10 MIN.)

W.1.2, W.1.7, L.1.1f

Student Objectives

I will be able to:
• Use an informational text planning guide.
• Understand how to provide closure for an informational text.
• Draft a closing statement for an informational text.

Additional Materials

• Writing portfolio
Presentation BLM 51
• Informational Report Planning Chart

Engage Thinking

Display the Informational Text Anchor Chart from Day 1 and review it with students.

Say: *A strong informational text has an introduction with strong and clear main idea. It gives the readers supporting facts and definitions. It also has a conclusion. Today we will plan our writing by deciding what facts we need to include in our informational report.*

Model

Use a think-aloud to model how to plan an informational report.

Sample think-aloud: *We have brainstormed topics and found supporting facts and definitions. I am going to write about my computer. Now I will plan my writing. I will write the big ideas I know I want to say about my computer and the supporting facts for each idea. I am going to use a planning chart to organize the key ideas and facts my informational report will present.*

Model filling out the Informational Report Planning chart with your class. Begin by modeling the selection of key ideas. Then write down the first two or three ideas and facts, then collaborate with your class to complete the planning chart. Point out that you are combining details from your research with facts you know from your own life.

• *When I plan, I write the topic of my informational text and the key ideas.*
• *Next, I write down the facts that support each idea. I don't worry about writing complete sentences. I just want to get my ideas written down on paper.*

Topic: Computer	
Key Ideas	**Facts**
My computer is a good.	• Goods are something people want or need. • Goods are things made, sold, and bought. • I need my computer. • I bought my computer.
My computer helps me work.	• Technology helps people work. • I use my computer to communicate to coworkers. • I use my computer to plan my lessons.
I use my computer for fun.	• I watch movies on my computer. • I go on social media with my computer. • I keep up with my friends and family online.

Sample Informational Report Planning Chart

Practice (iELD)

Have students work with a partner to complete the first step of the planning process: selecting key ideas. Remind students to listen to their partner's ideas and provide feedback that will help their partner plan his or her informational text. Tell students that this plan will help them during the writing process.

© Benchmark Education Company, LLC

Quick Write

Say: *Now it's your turn to write. Complete your plan by adding facts about the topic you chose. Remember, you do not need to write these facts as complete sentences. This is just the plan, and the important thing is to get all the facts you need in the places you need them.*

When students complete their plans, have them add the plan to their Informational Report portfolio.

Build Language Review: Adjectives

Remind students that they have been learning to use adjectives to describe people, places, and things. Tell students that, sometimes, more than one adjective can help us describe and object. When that happens, they can use commas to list the adjectives just the same way they would use comma to make a list of nouns.

Point to an object in the classroom and say a sentence using an adjective to describe it, such as, *This is a red book.*

Ask: *What other adjectives describe the book?*

Prompt students to help you write a list of adjectives to describe the book.

book
red
big
rectangular
interesting
sturdy

Prompt students to help you to create a description of the book that includes more than two adjectives. For example: *This book is red, sturdy, and rectangular.* Point out how commas are used to separate the adjectives in the list.

Oral Language Practice
Have partners find a classroom object and describe it with a sentence that uses more than two adjectives: *This _____ is _____, _____, and _____.*

W.1.2 Write informative/explanatory texts in which they name a topic, supply some facts about the topic, and provide some sense of closure. **W.1.7** Participate in shared research and writing projects (e.g. explore a number of "how-to" books on a given topic and use them to write a sequence of instructions). **L.1.1f** Use frequently occurring adjectives.

Informational Report: Write a Draft (10 MIN.) W.1.2, W.1.5, W.1.7, L.1.1f

Engage Thinking

Tell students that now that they have completed their planning, it is time to use their plans to help them write a draft of their informational text.

Say: *Let's review our planning chart before we begin.*

Topic: Computer	
Key Ideas	**Facts**
My computer is a good.	• Goods are something people want and need. • Goods are things made, sold, and bought. • I need my computer. • I bought my computer.
My computer helps me work.	• Technology helps people work. • I use my computer to communicate to coworkers. • I use my computer to plan my lessons.
I use my computer for fun.	• I watch movies on my computer. • I go on social media with my computer. • I keep up with my friends and family online.

Sample Informational Report Planning Chart

Model

Work with students to write a draft of your informational text. Point out that the draft should open with a statement of your most important idea. Show how the key ideas and supporting facts from the Informational Report Planning chart form the following sentences. As you write each sentence, model how you apply your knowledge of print concepts, phonics, high-frequency words, and English language conventions. Note, however, that this sample and your own model should include intentional errors and weakness to be improved later in the writing process.

> My computer is an important good that I use every day. A good is something that is made or grown and sold and bought. My laptop computer was built by a technology company. Bought it at the electronics store. Goods are also things that people need and want. I need my computer at work and at home. My computer helps me at work. I use it to e-mail my coworkers. Plan my daily lessons. My computer helps me at home. I use my computer to keep up with my family on social media and buy things I need. Finally, my computer is fun. I watch movies and television and videos on my computer.

Sample Informational Report Draft

Practice

Say: *Now turn to a partner and discuss how you will start your essay and what facts you will include to support your key ideas. Share your planning chart with your partner. Work together to help each other pick the strongest facts and organize your writing.*

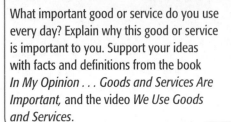

Student Writing Prompt

What important good or service do you use every day? Explain why this good or service is important to you. Support your ideas with facts and definitions from the book *In My Opinion . . . Goods and Services Are Important,* and the video *We Use Goods and Services*.

Student Objectives

I will be able to:
• Add details to an informational text.
• Use commas in a series.

Additional Materials

• Writing portfolios

Independent Writing

Provide time for students to write independently.

Students may write during writer's workshop time or at a writing station during small-group reading time. Independent Writing should occur before the Partner Share. Use the Build Language Review as needed while you confer and monitor.

 Confer and Monitor

As students write independently, support their efforts as needed using prompts like those provided here.

Directive Feedback: *Use your planning chart to keep you on track. Follow your plan!*

Self-Monitoring and Reflection: *Did you change your plan as you spoke with your partner or as you wrote? How do these changes improve your writing?*

Validating and Confirming: *Excellent draft! Your introduction is clear and your facts support your key ideas.*

Partner Share

Say: *Now let's share our drafts with a partner. While we share, let's practice our sharing skills: giving compliments, asking questions, and offering suggestions.*

Select a student as your partner and model one sharing skill. Monitor partners as they share their drafts and provide feedback. After students are done sharing, have them place their drafts in their Informational Text portfolios.

Build Language Review: Use Commas

Review the rules for commas in a series: in a series of three or more items, place a comma between every item and before the conjunction.

Organize the students into peer groups. Tell them to pretend that they are going to pack for a weekend camping trip. Have each group write down a series of four things that they would pack. Have groups share their ideas and write them down for the whole class to see. Ask the members of each group to help you identify where you should place the commas in their list of items.

Oral Language Practice

Have partners create four-item packing lists for a trip to the beach. Have each partner orally share their sentence and ask them to pause in order to indicate the commas in their response.

iELD Integrated ELD

Light Support
Display your Planning Chart and your model draft. Review you draft with students. For each sentence of support, ask volunteers to identify the detail in your planning that was the origin of each sentence. Check off each detail in your planning chart as it is used. Discuss with the group any unused details from your plan or new details you added as you wrote. Point out how your opening sentence is a summary of your key ideas.

Moderate Support
Display your Planning Chart and your model draft. Number each detail in your planning chart. Work with the group to identify where each detail was used in your draft. When the group identifies where a detail was used, write that detail's number near the first word of the sentence.

Substantial Support
Present as above, but focus specifically on the first key idea in your Planning Chart. Present students with a side-by-side presentation of the details from the Planning Chart and the sentence you created from that detail.

Detail from Planning Chart	Sentence from Draft
Goods are something people want and need.	Goods are also things that people need and want.
Goods are things made, sold, and bought.	A good is something that is made or grown and sold and bought. My computer was built by a technology company.
I need my computer.	I need my computer at work and at home.
I bought my computer.	I bought it at the electronics store.

Work with students to compare and contrast your drafted sentence with your original planning notes.

W.1.2 Write informative/explanatory texts in which they name a topic, supply some facts about the topic, and provide some sense of closure. **W.1.5** With guidance and support from adults, focus on a topic, respond to questions and suggestions from peers, and add details to strengthen writing as needed. **W.1.7** Participate in shared research and writing projects (e.g. explore a number of "how-to" books on a given topic and use them to write a sequence of instructions). **L.1.1f** Use commas in dates and to separate single words in a series.

Informational Report: Revise to Add a Conclusion and a Title (10 MIN.) W.1.2, W.1.7, L.1.2c

Engage Thinking

Remind students that a strong title gives readers an idea about what they are about to read and gets readers interested in reading more. A strong conclusion restates the writing's key ideas in a new and interesting way.

Say: *Now we are going to revise our writing to add a conclusion title to our writing.*

Model

Display the Draft Informational Report. Then model how to add a title and a conclusion.

Revised Informational Report Draft

Use think-alouds while you revise your draft:

- *I want a title that tells readers that my computer is an important good I use every day, but I also want it to express how much I like my computer.* I Love My Computer *is clear and shows readers how much I like my computer. I'll add an exclamation point for added emphasis.*
- *What are my key ideas? The computer is a good I use every day. I use it for work and I use it for fun.* Every day, I use my computer to make my work easier and my free time more interesting! *That makes it clear that I use my computer every day. It also reminds readers of the many ways the computer makes my life better. I think that is a strong ending.*

Practice (IELD)

Have partners discuss possible titles and discuss how to end their writing with a strong conclusion.

Say: *Listen carefully to your partner's ideas and feedback. If your partner thinks your title and conclusion are strong, so will other readers.*

Student Objectives

I will be able to:
- Revise an informational report.
- Use commas in dates.

Additional Materials

- Writing portfolios

Presentation BLM 52

- Commas in Dates Chart

Independent Writing

Provide time for students to write independently.

Students may write during writer's workshop time or at a writing station during small-group reading time. Independent Writing should occur before the Whole-Group Share. Use the Build Language Review as needed while you confer and monitor.

 Confer and Monitor

As students write independently, support their efforts as needed using prompts like those provided here.

Directive and Corrective Feedback: *What is the most important thing you want your reader to know about the good or service you picked. Use that detail to help make a strong title.*

Self-Monitoring and Reflection: *Does your writing help readers feel the way you do about the good or service you choose? How can you use the conclusion to communicate how you feel?*

Validating and Conferring: *Excellent! Your title makes me curious to read more, and your conclusion reminds me of your main idea, but it says it in a new way.*

Whole-Group Share

Model sharing your revised draft with the class, pointing out the title's connection to the rest of your writing and the new conclusion. Then ask volunteers to share their work with the class. Have them explain their new titles and show how their conclusions end their writing in a strong way. After students are done, have them place their revised drafts in their Informational Text portfolios.

Build Language Review: Use Commas

Remind students of the rules for using commas in representing dates. Display the following sample dates. Have partners work together to place commas in the proper places.

Nouns
July 17[,] 2011
Wednesday[,] April 6
Wednesday[,] April 6 [,] 2016

Sample Commas in Dates Chart

Oral Language Practice

Have partners create dates using the following sentence frames: *I will _____ on _____.* Encourage students to be creative with their dates. Partners should pause to indicate the commas in their dates.

W.1.2 Write informative/explanatory texts in which they name a topic, supply some facts about the topic, and provide some sense of closure. **W.1.7** Participate in shared research and writing projects (e.g. explore a number of "how-to" books on a given topic and use them to write a sequence of instructions). **L.1.2c** Use commas in dates and to separate single words in a series.

iELD Integrated ELD

Light Support
Have students discuss with their partner what they will label in their picture. Have them check the spelling of the items they want to label before they write, by looking in a source or reference book or asking a teacher.

Moderate Support
Support partners in labeling their pictures.
Say: *Tell your partner the parts of your picture you want to label. If you're not sure what to call something or how to spell the label, ask your partner first, and then check with me if you're still not sure.*

Substantial Support
Use the following prompts to help students label their picture.
Say: *What do you want to label? Point to it. Now tell me what you want to write on the label.*
Help students with language and spelling before they write.

Informational Report: Edit for Comma Use and Complete Sentences (10 MIN.) W.1.2, W.1.7, L.1.1f, L.1.2c

Engage Thinking

Say: *Writers always edit their texts before they share them. They ask themselves, "Did I write in complete sentence? Did I use my punctuation correctly?"*

Tell students that they are going to edit their texts. They should focus on eliminating any incomplete sentences. They also want to be sure they have used commas correctly.

Model

First, display your revisions and discuss the changes you made and why you made them.

- *The phrase* Bought it at the electronics store *is an incomplete sentence. It doesn't say who is doing the action of the verb. I am doing it. I'll add that and make it a complete sentence.*
- Plan my daily lessons *is not a complete sentence. I can make it one by using a conjunction and combining it to the previous sentence.*
- *I see another series! The second to the last sentence has a series of three things, and commas would be a better way to separate them.*

> **I Love My Computer!**
> **By _____**
> My computer is an important good that I use every day. A good is something that is made or grown and sold and bought. My laptop computer was built by a technology company. I bought it at the electronics store. Goods are also things that people need and want. I need my computer at work and at home. My computer helps me at work. I use it to e-mail my coworkers and plan my daily lessons. My computer helps me at home. I use my computer to keep up with my family on social media and buy things I need. Finally, my computer is fun. I watch movies, television, and videos on my computer. Every day, I use my computer to make my work easier and my free time more interesting!

Edited Informational Report Draft

Practice

Ask students to read their draft to their partners to eliminate sentence fragments and correct their use of commas. If students cannot find any incomplete sentences or punctuation errors, encourage them to check their spelling or correct other errors. Every student should find at least one way to improve his or her writing.

Independent Writing

Provide students with an opportunity to edit their writing.

Students may edit during writer's workshop time or at a writing station during small-group reading time. Independent Writing should occur before the Partner Share and Build Language Review.

Student Writing Prompt

What important good or service do you use every day? Explain why this good or service is important to you. Support your ideas with facts and definitions from the book *In My Opinion . . . Goods and Services Are Important* and the video *We Use Goods and Services.*

Student Objectives

I will be able to:
- Edit an informational report.
- Use common adjectives.

Additional Materials

- Writing portfolios

 **Confer and Monitor**

As students edit independently, support their efforts as needed using prompts like those provided here.

Directive Feedback: *Read each sentence of draft aloud, to yourself. Often you catch mistakes when reading your writing out loud.*

Self-Monitoring and Reflection: *When you are fixing an incomplete sentence, think about the different ways you can fix it. What best expresses what you are trying to say?*

Validating and Confirming: *I see that you corrected _____ and _____. That's careful editing, and it really improves your writing. Good work!*

Partner Share

Say: *Now let's share our writing with a partner. Read your writing aloud. Talk with your partner about the edits you made and how they improved your writing.*

Monitor partners as they share their writing. After students have shared, have them place their edited writings in their Informational Text portfolios.

Build Language Review: Adjectives

Remind students that an adjective is a word that describes a person, place, or thing.

Form students into peer groups. Ask one student to think of a character from one of the folktales they've read in class. They should share adjectives that describe that character with their group, without telling the group what character they are describing. After each adjective they share, the group should guess what character the student is describing.

Let multiple students have the opportunity to describe a secret character.

After the groups have had a chance to describe and guess characters, have them share their efforts with the class. How many adjectives did the group need to guess that character? What adjective gave the character away?

Oral Language Practice
Have students describe one of the characters from any story they have read in class. The student's description must include at least three adjectives. For example: *Little Red Riding Hood is young and forgetful. She is lucky she wasn't eaten.*

 **Integrated ELD**

Light Support
Work with the group to create a list of comma use rules. Have students copy out this list and use it to check their revised drafts.

Moderate Support
Review the use of commas in dates and series.
Ask: *Do we need to fix anything in this sentence? What do we need to fix?*

> Our flag is red white and blue.
> Today is August 3 2016

Once students understand the use of commas, tell them to edit their drafts, with a partner using the same routine: read each sentence with a comma or commas in it, check to see if corrections are needed, then make changes if necessary.

Substantial Support
Review the use of commas in dates and series. Work with students to correct the following sentences.

> Our flag is red white and blue.
> Today is August 3 2016

Once the group has corrected the commas, explain the rules for each situation and point out how each sentence was revised to comply with these rules.

W.1.2 Write informative/explanatory texts in which they name a topic, supply some facts about the topic, and provide some sense of closure. **W.1.7** Participate in shared research and writing projects (e.g. explore a number of "how-to" books on a given topic and use them to write a sequence of instructions). **L.1.1f** Use frequently occurring adjectives. **L.1.2c** Use commas in dates and to separate single words in a series.

Informational Report: Publish the Report (10 MIN.) W.1.2, W.1.7, L.1.1f

Engage Thinking

Remind students that in the last two weeks, you have been working together to write informational reports. Display and reread the Informational Report Mentor Text. When you finish, spend a few moments reviewing the processes you went through to plan, draft, revise, and edit your informational text.

I Love My Computer!

By _____

My computer is an important good that I use every day. A good is something that is made or grown and sold and bought. My laptop computer was built by a technology company. I bought it at the electronics store. Goods are also things that people need and want. I need my computer at work and at home. My computer helps me at work. I use it to e-mail my coworkers and plan my daily lessons. My computer helps me at home. I use my computer to keep up with my family on social media and buy things I need. Finally, my computer is fun. I watch movies, television, and videos on my computer. Every day, I use my computer to make my work easier and my free time more interesting!

Sample Informational Report Mentor Text

Say: *This is the published version the informational report I wrote about my computer. I even used my computer to published it! You do not need a computer to create a finished, published piece of writing. You can also publish your work by writing a neat, error-free final copy.*

Create a Publishing Checklist

Say: *Before you publish your work, let's make a publishing checklist that will help you make sure that your finished work has everything a published piece of writing should have.*

Work with students to create a publishing checklist for digital and handwritten publication. You may ignore the row for adding supporting images, depending on whether you asked students to execute their plans to add supporting photographs.

Feature	Computer	Handwritten
title at top		
author's name under title		
special font for title and author		
clear handwriting		
correct spacing		
supporting images (optional)		

Sample Publishing Checklist

Student Writing Prompt

What important good or service do you use every day? Explain why this good or service is important to you. Support your ideas with facts and definitions from the book *In My Opinion . . . Goods and Services Are Important,* and the video *We Use Goods and Services*.

Student Objectives

I will be able to:
• Make a final version of my informational text.

Additional Materials

• Writing portfolios
Presentation BLM 53
• Publishing Checklist

Peer Collaboration

Have students read their final drafts aloud to a partner and decide how they're going to publish their informational texts. Students should discuss the benefits and drawbacks of each form of publishing.

Publication

Students may publish during writer's workshop time or at a writing station during small-group reading time. Remind students to put their published pieces in their Informational Text portfolios.

Build Language Review: Adjectives

Work with the class to identify adjectives from the mentor text. In the sample text provided, the adjectives include the following.

Sentence	Adjective(s)	Modified Noun(s)
My computer is an important good that I use every day.	important	good
My laptop computer was built by a technology company.	laptop	computer
My computer helps me at work. I use it to e-mail my coworkers and plan my daily lessons.	daily	lessons
Finally, my computer is fun.	fun	computer

Call on volunteers to identify sentences from their own writing that include adjectives. Work with the class to add them to your list.

Oral Language Practice

Have partners find an adjective in their own writing and read the sentence aloud. If they cannot find an adjective in their own writing, have them discuss with their partner and identify where an adjective could be added.

iELD Integrated ELD

Light Support
Have students use the Publishing Checklist to review their text. Then have them write or type their final copy. When their final copy is complete, have them read it aloud one last time to a partner. Explain that reading aloud is a great way to check for any remaining errors. If they stumble over any parts, they may need to check for correct punctuation, spelling, or neatness.

Moderate Support
Have students use the Publishing Checklist to review their text. Then have them write or type their final copy. When their final copy is complete, have them read it aloud one last time to a partner as you monitor. Explain that reading aloud is a great way to check for any remaining errors. If they stumble over any parts, point out that they may need to check for correct punctuation, spelling, or neatness.

Substantial Support
Have students use the Publishing Checklist to review their text. Then have them write or type their final copy with assistance as needed. When their final copy is complete, have them read it aloud to you one last time. Explain that reading aloud is a great way to check for any remaining errors such as spelling, punctuation, and neatness. If errors are identified, help them fix them on their final copy.

W.1.2 Write informative/explanatory texts in which they name a topic, supply some facts about the topic, and provide some sense of closure. **W.1.7** Participate in shared research and writing projects (e.g. explore a number of "how-to" books on a given topic and use them to write a sequence of instructions). **L.1.1f** Use frequently occurring adjectives.

© Benchmark Education Company, LLC

Grade 1 · Unit 9 · Week 3   **119**

Informational Report: Share the Report (10 MIN.) W.1.2, W.1.7, SL.1.1b, SL.1.2

Engage Thinking

Display the Mentor Text.

Say: *Today we will share our informational reports with a partner. I will show you how to give compliments, ask questions, and give suggestions to your partner.*

I Love My Computer!

By _____

My computer is an important good that I use every day. A good is something that is made or grown and sold and bought. My laptop computer was built by a technology company. I bought it at the electronics store. Goods are also things that people need and want. I need my computer at work and at home. My computer helps me at work. I use it to e-mail my coworkers and plan my daily lessons. My computer helps me at home. I use my computer to keep up with my family on social media and buy things I need. Finally, my computer is fun. I watch movies, television, and videos on my computer. Every day, I use my computer to make my work easier and my free time more interesting!

Informational Report Mentor Text

Model Peer Collaboration

Read aloud your published informational report. Then ask a volunteer to introduce and read aloud his or her work to you. After reading, model how you give the writer a compliment using sentence frames such as:

- *I liked how you _____.*
- *I thought that _____ really supported what you were saying.*
- *I understood _____ better because you _____.*
- *I enjoyed the part _____.*

Remind students that compliments should be specific to the writer's work. You want to point out exactly what you liked about his or her writing. Tell students that compliments are kind. The writers work hard on their work so it is rude to make them feel bad about it:

Have students share their work with their partners and give students time to give each other compliments.

Next, return to your volunteer partner and practice asking him or her a question. Remind students that, as with the compliment, it is important to be kind and specific. Tell students that the goal of asking questions is to get the writer to think about ways they can improve his or her work. After reading, model asking a question using the following sentence frames:

- *Out of all the topics your brainstormed, why did you pick this topic?*
- *What fact did you find most interesting about your topic?*
- *What do you think is the most challenging part of the writing process?*

Finally model offering suggestions with your volunteer partner. Remind students that suggestions should be said in a nice way, should be specific, and are meant to help the writer improve his or her writing next time they write. Use the following sentence stems to help you model offering suggestions:

- _____ *seems like a really important key idea, and I'd like to read more facts about it.*
- *I think _____ would help the readers understand how important these details are.*
- *You should _____ with the conclusion to let your readers understand how you feel about the topic.*

Practice Peer Collaboration

Invite students to read their published writing to their partners and practice the three sharing skills they have learned. Monitor students as they share their writing and feedback.

Whole-Group Share

Select a few student volunteers to read their informational reports to the whole class. Invite classmates to give compliments, ask questions, and make suggestions. Remind them that the writer should respond by saying "Thank you" and/or answering the question.

Place the informational reports in your classroom library for students to reread throughout the school year. Alternatively, allow students to take their portfolios home or file them to use as documentation of students' developing writing skills.

iELD Integrated ELD

Light Support
Have partners take turns reading the Mentor Text aloud. Have them practice each of the three sharing skills: giving a compliment, asking a question, and offering a suggestion. Have partners work together to ensure that their feedback is kind, specific, and helpful.

Moderate Support
Have students echo-read the Mentor Text. Have students give compliments, ask questions, and give suggestions. Encourage them to use sentence frames:
I like how you _____.
Why did you decide to _____?
I think your writing would be even stronger if you _____.

Substantial Support
Have students echo-read the Mentor Text. Assist students in giving compliments about the text. Encourage them to use sentence frame *I like _____.*

W.1.2 Write informative/explanatory texts in which they name a topic, supply some facts about the topic, and provide some sense of closure. **W.1.7** Participate in shared research and writing projects (e.g. explore a number of "how-to" books on a given topic and use them to write a sequence of instructions). **SL.1.1b** Build on others' talk in conversations by responding to the comments of others through multiple exchanges. **SL.1.2** Ask and answer questions about key details in a text read aloud or information presented orally or through other media.

Introduce the Genre: Acrostic Poems

(15 MIN.) RL.1.10

Student Objectives

I will be able to:
- Learn that an acrostic poem uses the letters of a topic word to start each line of the poem.
- Listen to an acrostic poem read aloud and identify the features.
- Contribute lines for a class acrostic poem.

Additional Materials

- Chart paper
- Writing portfolios

Engage Thinking

Tell students that they are going to learn about a kind of poem called an acrostic poem. Explain that the first letter of each line, when read from top to bottom, spells out a word. Often the word is a name, but it can also be a place, object, or idea. That word tells the topic of the poem, and the poem describes the topic. Tell students that this week you will work together to read and write an acrostic poem.

Read the Mentor Text

Display and read aloud the following mentor text. When you finish, allow students to respond with comments or questions.

Say: *After reading the title, most people start reading an acrostic poem by looking at the first letter of each line and then reading these letters from top to bottom to see what they spell. This word is the topic of the acrostic poem. The letters here spell out "Sounds." This tells me that this acrostic poem is about sounds.*

Sounds

Shriek! Bark! Crunch! Hiss! Pop! Thud!

Over, in, around, and

Under things.

Noises are everywhere!

Do you want peace and quiet?

Shhhhh!

Acrostic Poem Mentor Text

Analyze the Mentor Text

Say: *Let's use this text to analyze the features of an acrostic poem.*

As you go through the text, point out the following features and list them on a chart. Explain to students that they can refer to this chart throughout the week.

An acrostic poem . . .

- has a title that is often the same as the topic word
- has one line for each letter of the topic word
- has a capital letter at the beginning of each line
- can have one word or many words per line
- can sometimes have ideas that carry over to the next line
- can have complete or incomplete sentences
- uses different types of punctuation
- uses strong, vivid words and phrases

Acrostic Poem Anchor Chart

Point out to students that reading an acrostic poem aloud is different from reading a story or an informational text. For example: I read more slowly because I have to pay attention to punctuation. I pause for commas and periods. I change my voice when I see an exclamation point or a question mark.

Model

Explain to students that you will work together to write a class acrostic poem about light. Model how to set up the poem, writing **Light** from top to bottom on the board and showing how to fill in line 1. For example: *I want to tell about light. What gives light? A lamp gives light. I will write that in line 1.* Have students help you think of ideas for lines 2 and 3.

> **Light**
> **L**amps give light.
> **I**n the sky, the sun
> **G**leams and glows.
> **H**eadlights move along the highway at night.
> **T**winkle, twinkle little star!

Sample Acrostic Poem Practice Text

Practice

Have students work in partners to rewrite the first three lines of the practice text. Remind them to check the anchor chart if they need help. Have them practice reading the first three lines to their partners, paying attention to punctuation and varying their voice.

 **Quick Write** (iELD)

Have students work independently to write lines for the letters H and T. Remind them that they can use a single word, an incomplete sentence, or a complete sentence, but whatever they write must relate to the topic of light.

Present Portfolios

Hand out prepared portfolios.

Say: *Here is a portfolio you may use to store all the writing you do for the sensory poem. This will help you organize your work and ideas so you can refer to them when needed.*

Allow time for students to write their names on their portfolios, file their quick writes, and store the portfolios in a designated spot in the classroom.

(iELD) Integrated ELD

Light Support
For ideas, encourage students to make a list of different types and sources of light they see in their everyday lives.

Moderate Support
Display sentence frames for students to use. For example:
- *Some words that begin with the letter [H or T] are* _____.
- *I can say* _____ *to tell something about light.*

Substantial Support
Carry out the Moderate Support activity but provide extra support by helping students brainstorm words and modeling ways to use these in the lines of the poem.

RL.1.10 With prompting and support, read prose and poetry of appropriate complexity for grade 1.

Brainstorm Ideas for an Acrostic Poem (15 MIN.) RL.1.10, W.1.5

Engage Thinking

Remind students that when they brainstorm, they come up with ideas for what they want to write about. Briefly review the Acrostic Poem Anchor Chart.

Say: *We learned that, in an acrostic poem, the first letters of each line from top to bottom spell out a word. This word tells the topic of the poem. Often acrostic poems use people's names as the topic, and the poem describes the person. Today you will brainstorm ideas for an acrostic poem about yourself.*

Model Brainstorm

Model how to brainstorm ideas for an acrostic poem using a think-aloud.

Sample think-aloud: *I'll write about my first-grade teacher. Her name was Mrs. Patricia Cather. I will think of words and phrases that describe Mrs. Cather. I'll think of what she was like and what she looked like. I'll also think of what she taught me at school, and what she liked to do when we weren't in school. Thinking about these things will help me brainstorm ideas for my acrostic poem.*

Model how to record your ideas on the board. For example:

Mrs. Cather
• kind
• creative
• funny
• tall
• wore glasses
• taught me many things
• found books she thought I would like
• treated everyone fairly
• told stories about her family
• liked to play tennis

Sample Brainstorming List

Read the completed list aloud.

Say: *I probably won't use every word and phrase in my poem, but I wanted to write all the ideas I could think of. This way, I can see which words and phrases might fit in my poem when I draft it. Some of the words might have the right letter to use at the beginning of a line. Some of the words might appear in other places.*

Remind students that they will write acrostic poems about themselves. Have them start brainstorming words and phrase they can use to describe themselves. Suggest that they begin with words and phrases that describe what they look like and what hobbies they do when they're not in school.

Practice

Have students work in partners to share their ideas about the descriptive words and phrases they brainstormed. Invite partners to brainstorm other suggestions by thinking about what activities they enjoy at school or what games or sports they play with their friends.

☑ Quick Write

Have students work independently to record their brainstormed ideas in a list using words and/or drawings. Remind them to file their work in their writing portfolios.

(iELD) Integrated ELD

Light Support

Write categories on the board to help students come up with ideas. For example:

- *what I look like*
- *what I act like*
- *things I like to do at school*
- *things I like to do at home*
- *things I collect*
- *places I like to go*

Moderate Support

Provide sentence frames for students to use as they describe themselves to a partner. For example:

- *I _____.*
- *I am _____.*
- *I can _____.*
- *I like to _____.*
- *I have _____.*

Substantial Support

Encourage students to write words in their own languages or make sketches of their ideas. Provide the sentence frames above for them to use as they verbalize their ideas.

RL.1.10 With prompting and support, read prose and poetry of appropriate complexity for grade 1. **W.1.5** With guidance and support from adults, focus on a topic, respond to questions and suggestions from peers, and add details to strengthen writing as needed.

Draft an Acrostic Poem (15 MIN.) W.1.5

Engage Thinking

Briefly review the structural features of an acrostic poem—a title that is often the same as the topic, one line for each letter of the topic word, a capital letter at the beginning of each line—by referring to the anchor chart. Tell students that they will now draft their acrostic poem about themselves.

Say: *You have brainstormed lists of words and phrases that describe yourselves. These lists will help you draft your acrostic poem. Your acrostic poem is about your name, so you know what the first letter of each line will be and you know how many lines your poem will have. Now you have to find the words and phrases that match the letters in your name. It's almost like putting together a puzzle. You match what you want to say with the letters and lines available in your name.*

Model

Tell students that you will draft the acrostic poem about your teacher Mrs. Cather. As you write each line, model how you apply your knowledge of print concepts, phonics, high-frequency words, and English language conventions. For example: *I first set up my draft by writing Mrs. Cather's first name, Patricia, in all uppercase letters from top to bottom on the left side of the page. I saw that I had eight lines in my poem, and I saw which letters begin the first word in each line. Then I used my brainstorming list to help me figure out what to write about Mrs. Cather.*

> **Mrs. Cather**
> **P**layed tennis.
> **A**lways kind and fair.
> **T**all with glasses.
> "**R**ead this! You will love it!"
> **I** liked her funny stories.
> **C**reative teacher.
> **I** will always remember her.
> **A** role model for me!

Acrostic Poem Draft

Display your brainstorming list. Think aloud as you read through it, circling words and phrases you used in your poem.

Sample think-aloud: *The first letter in "Patricia" is a P, and I wrote "liked to play tennis" in my list. I changed it to the word **Played** to match the letter P. For letter A, I wanted to tell that Mrs. Cather was kind and fair, but the letters K and F aren't in her name. So, I thought of a word that begins with the letter A that would help describe how kind and fair she was. I used the word **Always**, so that line now says: "Always kind and fair."*

Explain that you didn't use all the ideas on the brainstorming list, and you added words and phrases to include new ideas or help the lines come out right. For example, point out that the fourth line shows something Mrs. Cather often said, and the last line has the new phrase "role model" that you thought of.

Student Objectives

I will be able to:
• Use a brainstorming list to draft an acrostic poem.
• Follow the structure of an acrostic poem while drafting.
• Share my draft with a partner.

Additional Materials
• Writing portfolios

Practice

Have students work in partners to set up their drafts with their name written from top to bottom in all uppercase letters. Explain that if students' first names are very short, they might want to add their middle or last names to the poem so they will have more letters to work with. Conversely, if their first names are very long, they might want to use a nickname. Then have them take out their brainstorming lists and work together to circle the words and phrases that match the letters in their name.

Independent Writing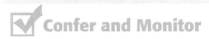

Have students work independently to write their drafts using the work they did with their partners. Remind them to use their brainstorming lists, but that they can add new words or phrases whenever they like. Tell them to save their drafts in their writing portfolios.

Students may write during writer's workshop time or at a writing station during small-group reading time. Independent Writing should occur before the Partner Share activity.

☑ Confer and Monitor

As students write independently, support their efforts as needed using prompts such as:

Directive Feedback: *You use this word to describe yourself on your brainstorming list. It begins with the letter _____. This letter is also in your name, so maybe you could use the word here.*

Self-Monitoring and Reflection: *Could you put these two ideas together on the same line? What word could you use at the beginning of the line that begins with the letter _____?*

Validating and Confirming: *I like how you use one word on this line and a sentence on this line. This makes the poem interesting to read.*

Partner Share

Ask students to share their drafts with a partner. If their poem doesn't yet have a title, ask the partners to come up with one together. Remind them that the title can be the same as the topic word (the student's name), or it can be different. However, it must relate to something in the poem.

iELD Integrated ELD

Light Support
Before students begin writing their lines, check to make sure they've set up their poems correctly, with their names written vertically in all uppercase letters on the left side of the paper.

Moderate Support
Work with students to set up their poems, with their names spelled vertically on the paper. Remind them to refer to their brainstorming lists for ideas for each line.

Substantial Support
Help individual students set up their drafts. Then, referring to their brainstorming lists, help them come up with possible ideas using the following sentence frames:

• *My topic word is [name].*

• *The word _____ begins with the letter _____.*

• *A word/phrase/sentence that tells something about me is _____.*

W.1.5 With guidance and support from adults, focus on a topic, respond to questions and suggestions from peers, and add details to strengthen writing as needed.

Revise an Acrostic Poem (15 MIN.) W.1.5

Engage Thinking

Remind students that they wrote acrostic poems about themselves. Briefly review and discuss the last line of the Acrostic Poem Anchor Chart.

Say: *When we revise a draft, we can make it even stronger. I'll reread the draft of my acrostic poem about Mrs. Cather and see if I can revise any of my descriptions by adding words or changing words, such as nouns, verbs, and adjectives.*

Model

Work with students to revise your acrostic poem. As you write each sentence, model how you apply your knowledge of print concepts, phonics, high-frequency words and English language conventions.

> **Mrs. Cather**
> **P**layed tennis.
> **A**lways ~~kind~~ caring and fair.
> **T**all with glasses.
> "**R**ead this book! You will love it!"
> **I** ~~liked~~ laughed at her funny stories.
> **C**reative teacher.
> **I** will always remember her.
> **A** role model for me!

Acrostic Poem Draft

Model how to replace one adjective for a stronger adjective, change a verb to a more descriptive phrase, and add a noun to clarify ideas. Have students listen as you think aloud.

Sample think-aloud: *I'll change the word **kind** to the word **caring** in line 2. **Caring** is a more specific adjective, and I like the way it sounds with the word **fair**. In line 4, I'll add the noun **book** so it will say, "Read this book!" This helps my readers visualize Mrs. Cather handing me a book she knows I will enjoy. Then, in the next line, I'll replace the verb **liked** with the phrase "laughed at." **Liked** is a little boring, but now my readers know that Mrs. Cather's stories were so funny that they made me laugh.*

Practice

Have students work in partners to share and review their acrostic poem drafts. Suggest that partners circle or highlight places where they could add or change a noun, verb, or adjective to make their poem stronger.

Independent Writing

Have students independently revise their drafts, changing or adding a verb, a noun, or an adjective to make their poem stronger. Remind them to save their drafts in their writing portfolios.

Students may write during writer's workshop time or at a writing station during small-group reading time. Independent Writing should occur before the Whole-Group Share activity.

 Confer and Monitor

As students revise independently, support their efforts as needed using prompts such as:

Directive Feedback: *This is an adjective that we hear every day. Think of an adjective that means the same thing but sounds more interesting.*

Self-Monitoring and Reflection: *I see that you circled this line. Have you thought of a stronger way to say this? Do you want to add or change a word?*

Validating and Confirming: *I like how you replaced the word **fast** with the word **speedy**. This verb is much more specific and vivid. Good thinking!*

Whole-Group Share

Say: *Now let's share our writing with the group. Remember our classroom rules as you and your classmates share your writing.*

Model reading aloud your draft to the class. Point out the revisions you made. Select a few students to share their drafts. Monitor students as they share their thinking and writing. Invite students to give compliments, ask questions, and make suggestions about each other's work.

iELD Integrated ELD

Light Support
Have students put a star beside one or two lines they would like to make stronger. **Ask:** *What word or words could you add or change to help your readers picture this in their minds?*

Moderate Support
Help students choose one or two lines they would like to make stronger. Then have them analyze each line, using the following sentence frames:

- *The word/phrase _____ doesn't sound very interesting.*
- *I could add the word _____/change the word _____ to _____ to make the line stronger.*

Substantial Support
Work individually with students to choose a line of the poem to strengthen. Help them brainstorm ideas. Then offer the following sentence frames to help them verbalize their ideas:

- *I used the noun/verb/adjective _____.*
- *Some stronger words are _____.*
- *I will use the word(s) _____ in my poem.*

W.1.5 With guidance and support from adults, focus on a topic, respond to questions and suggestions from peers, and add details to strengthen writing as needed.

Publish and Share an Acrostic Poem (15 MIN.) W.1.5, W.1.6

Engage Thinking

Remind students that you have worked together to write acrostic poems. Display and read aloud your draft. When you finish, spend a few minutes to review the steps of brainstorming, drafting, and revising your work.

Student Objectives

I will be able to:
- Correct my draft to create a final version of my acrostic poem.
- Compliment, question, and make suggestions on a partner's acrostic poem.
- Share my acrostic poem with the class.

Additional Materials
- Writing portfolios

> **Mrs. Cather**
> **By** _____
> **P**layed tennis.
> **A**lways caring and fair.
> **T**all with glasses.
> "**R**ead this book! You will love it!"
> **I** laughed at her funny stories.
> **C**reative teacher.
> **I** will always remember her.
> **A** role model for me!

Acrostic Poem Draft

Say: *Now you will publish your work so that you can share it with each other and other people. I published my poem by typing it on a word processing program on a computer. You can also publish your poem by writing a neat, final copy. After we have finished publishing our work, we will practice giving a compliment, asking a question, and offering a suggestion to a partner on their acrostic poem.*

Publication

Review with students the process steps of publication: listing a title at the top, writing the author's name below the title, using a darker font for the title and the author, printing clearly, and correcting spacing. Have students decide how they are going to publish their acrostic poems. Students may publish during writer's workshop time or at a writing station during small-group reading time.

Model Peer Collaboration

Read aloud your published acrostic poem. Then ask a student to introduce their acrostic poem and read it aloud. After reading, model how you give the student a compliment using a sentence frame such as:

- *I like how you _____ because it made me visualize _____.*
- *My favorite line was _____ because _____.*
- *It was really interesting when _____ and I liked that because _____.*

Remind students that compliments can be about any part of the work, but they should always describe something positive and point to something specific in the writer's work.

Allow partners to read their acrostic poem and give each other compliments.

Next, model asking questions. Return to your student-partner's poem and model asking questions with sentence frames such as:

- *When we were brainstorming topics, what helped you think of that word or phrase?*
- *What revision do you think made the biggest difference to your writing?*
- *What was the hardest part about writing your acrostic poem?*

Point out that questions can be about the details of the writer's work or about how the writer created their acrostic poem. Either way, the questions should be friendly and focus on an important aspect of writing.

Allow students time to ask their partner questions.

Finally, model offering a suggestion. Return to your student-partner's acrostic poem and model offering your partner a suggestion to improve their writing. Use the following samples to help craft your own suggestion.

- *Adding a picture about something different that you do might help the reader understand what that activity is.*
- *It would be interesting to learn why you chose that verb to describe that action.*
- *I would love to know what your favorite part of your acrostic poem is.*

Explain to students that suggestions must be kind, specific to the text, and helpful to the writer. Review your own modeled suggestion and point out how it meets this criteria.

Allow time for students to review their partner's work and offer suggestions.

Practice Peer Collaboration

Invite partners to read their published acrostic poems aloud and give compliments, ask questions, and make suggestions about each other's work.

Whole-Group Share (iELD)

Select a few students to share their acrostic poems with the whole group. Invite class members to give compliments, ask questions, and make suggestions about each other's work. Remind them to thank each other for compliments and suggestions, and to answer questions that their listeners might ask.

After everyone has shared, briefly discuss the acrostic poem writing process, how students feel about it, and what they have learned as writers.

Place the acrostic poems in your classroom library for students to reread throughout the rest of the school year. Alternatively, allow students to take their portfolios home and/or file them to use as documentation of students' developing writing skills.

(iELD) Integrated ELD

Light Support
Quickly review the concepts of compliments, questions, and suggestions before students engage in the whole-group sharing activity.

Moderate Support
Provide sentence frames to help students with their compliments, questions, and suggestions. For example:

- *I like . . .*
- *I notice . . .*
- *How did you . . .*
- *What are the . . .*
- *Maybe you could . . .*
- *You might like to . . .*

Substantial Support
Provide the sentence frames in the Moderate Support activity, but model an example of each type of feedback to further support students as they respond to classmates' sharing.

W.1.5 With guidance and support from adults, focus on a topic, respond to questions and suggestions from peers, and add details to strengthen writing as needed. **W.1.6** With guidance and support from adults, use a variety of digital tools to produce and publish writing, including in collaboration with peers.

Reflect on Narrative Writing (10 MIN.) W.1.3

Engage Thinking

Briefly review the narrative writing assignments students have completed this school year—stories, folktales, new story endings, dialogues, plays, journal entries, notes, first person character narratives, and personal narratives.

Say: *Today we're going to think about our narrative writing. We'll begin by reviewing the features of narrative writing that we've worked on throughout the school year.*

Share the Rubric

Display and read aloud the narrative writing rubric.

Say: *This is a rubric. A rubric is a list of features and characteristics that tells us what a strong example of narrative writing should have. Writers should include all of the things on the rubric in their narrative writing.*

Discuss each item on the rubric with the class. Make sure that all your students understand what each element of the rubric describes.

A strong narrative includes . . .
Two or more events in a sequence.
Details about what happened.
Words that signal the order of events.
An end that provides a sense of closure.

Narrative Writing Rubric

Reread Narratives

> **Management Tip:** You may let each student choose a narrative to review and share or, in the interest of managing time, you may choose to select an exemplary representative of each student's work prior to class time.

Hand out students' narrative writing portfolios and invite them to reread their work. Distribute copies of the rubric.

Say: *Use the rubric as you read to evaluate your writing. What narrative did you write that includes every item on our rubric? Which narratives have especially strong examples of an item on the rubric?*

Have students pick out the narrative they think does the best job of including every element in the rubric. Explain to students that they will be sharing this writing with a partner.

Student Objectives

I will be able to:
• Review the features of narrative writing.
• Reflect on my own narrative writing.

Additional Materials

• Writing portfolios

Peer Rehearsal

Match students with a partner and have each student explain how the writing they selected includes the elements in the rubric.

Say: *Now read your writing to your partner. When you are done, point out where you included each of the different elements from the rubric. If there is an element that you did not include in the writing, work with your partner to think of how it might have been included. After you have shared your writing, listen as your partner shares his or hers.*

Share Your Understanding

Invite volunteers to share observations about their narrative writing. Remind them that reflection is different from editing, revising, and peer review. Instead, it is a way to think about our own writing in a new way. Provide the following sentence stems to assist students as they share:

- *This was my first time to write a _____.*
- *I like that I _____.*
- *I wish that I _____.*
- *I especially enjoyed writing _____ because _____.*
- *I didn't really enjoy writing _____ because _____.*

Write a Compliment

On the bottom of their rubrics, ask students to write a compliment to themselves about something they feel they do well as a narrative writer.

iELD Integrated ELD

Light Support
Allow students to work with on-level partners to complete the rubric.

Moderate Support
Review the meanings of vocabulary words on the rubric, such as **sequence, signal**, and **closure**, as you go through the statements as a group.

Substantial Support
Work one-on-one with students to complete the rubric. Read each statement aloud and help the student locate an example of the skill (or a place where the skill could be used) in his or her narrative writing.

W.1.3 Write narratives in which they recount two or more appropriately sequenced events, include some details regarding what happened, use temporal words to signal event order, and provide some sense of closure.

Reflect on Informational Text Writing W.1.2, SL.1.4

Engage Thinking

Briefly review the informational text writing assignments students have completed this school year–key details, ideas, and events; descriptions and explanations; compare-contrast texts; series of events; a time line; rules and lists; and answers to questions about texts they've read.

Say: *Now we're going to think about our informational text writing. We'll begin by reviewing the features of informational text writing that we've worked on throughout the school year.*

Share the Rubric

Display and read aloud the informational text writing rubric.

Say: *This is another rubric. This rubric is a little different than the last one you used because this rubric is meant to be used with informational texts and reports. It lists features and characteristics that strong examples of narrative writing should have.*

Discuss each item on the rubric with the class. Make sure that all your students understand what each element of the rubric describes.

A strong informational text includes . . .
A clear topic.
Facts about the topic.
A conclusion that gives a sense of closure.

Informational Text Writing Rubric

Reread Informational Texts

Management Tip: As with the previous writing lesson's sharing, you may let each student choose an informational text to share or, in the interest of managing the available time, you may choose to select an exemplary representative of the student's work before the class begins.

Hand out students' informational text portfolios and invite them to reread their work. Distribute copies of the rubric.

Say: *Use the rubric as you read to evaluate your writing. What informational text or report did you write that includes every item on our rubric? Do you have any informational texts or reports that include especially strong examples of an item on the rubric?*

Have students pick out the informational text or report they think does the best job of including every element in the rubric. Explain to students that they will be sharing this writing with a partner.

Student Objectives

I will be able to:
• Review the features of informative/explanatory writing.
• Reflect on my own informative/explanatory writing.
• Share my reflections with others.

Additional Materials

• Writing Portfolios

Peer Rehearsal

Match students with a partner and have each student explain how the writing they selected includes the elements in the rubric.

Say: *Now read your informational text to your partner. When you are done, point out where you included each of the different elements from the rubric. If there is an element that you did not include in the writing, work with your partner to think of how it might have been included. After you are done sharing your writing, listen carefully as your partner shares his or her work.*

Share Your Understanding

Invite volunteers to share observations about their informational writing. Remind them that reflection is different from editing, revising, and peer review. Instead, it is a way to think about our own writing in a new way. Provide the following sentence stems to assist students as they share:

- *This was my first time to write a _____.*
- *I like that I _____.*
- *I wish that I _____.*
- *I especially enjoyed writing _____ because _____.*
- *I didn't really enjoy writing _____ because _____*

Write a Question

On the bottom of their rubrics, ask students to write a question they have about one of their informational pieces. Remind students that questions should be specific to the writing and focus on important details or elements of the piece or the writing process.

iELD Integrated ELD

Light Support
Allow students to work with on-level partners to complete the rubric.

Moderate Support
Review the meanings of vocabulary words on the rubric, such as **topic, facts,** and **closure** as you go through the statements as a group.

Substantial Support
Work one-on-one with students to complete the rubric. Read each statement aloud and help the student locate an example of the skill (or a place where the skill could be used) in his or her informative/explanatory writing.

W.1.2 Write informative/explanatory texts in which they name a topic, supply some facts about the topic, and provide some sense of closure. **SL.1.4** Describe people, places, things, and events with relevant details, expressing ideas and feelings clearly.

Reflect on Opinion Writing W.1.1, SL.1.4

Engage Thinking

Briefly review the opinion writing assignments students have completed this school year—opinions about rules, people's contributions, story characters, story illustrations, text features, inventions, sounds, activities, and texts they've read.

Say: *Let's reflect on, or think about, our opinion writing. We'll begin by reviewing the features of opinion writing that we've worked on throughout the school year.*

Share the Rubric

Display and read aloud the opinion text writing rubric.

Say: *This is a rubric that is specifically for opinion writings. Let's look at the features and characteristics it says a strong opinion piece will must have.*

Discuss each item on the rubric with the class. Make sure that all your students understand what each element of the rubric describes.

A strong opinion writing includes . . .
An introduction.
A clearly stated opinion.
Details that support the opinion.
Reasons for the opinion.
A conclusion that provides closure.

Opinion Writing Rubric

Reread Opinion Texts

Management Tip: As with the previous writing lesson's sharing, you may let each student choose an opinion piece or, to better manage class time, you may pre-select an exemplary representative of the student's work.

Hand out students' opinion writing portfolios and invite them to reread their work. Distribute copies of the rubric.

Say: *Use the rubric as you read to evaluate your writing. What opinion piece has everything on our rubric? Do you have an opinion piece you think you did an especially great job on?*

Have students pick out the opinion writing they think best fits the requirements of the rubric. Explain to students that they will be sharing this writing with a partner.

Student Objectives

I will be able to:
• Review the features of opinion writing.
• Reflect on my own opinion writing.
• Share my reflections with others.

Additional Materials

• Writing portfolios

Peer Rehearsal

Match students with a partner and have each student explain how the writing they selected includes the elements in the rubric.

Say: *Now read your opinion piece to your partner. When you are done, point out where you included each of the different elements from the rubric. What if you find there is an element on the rubric that you did not include in your writing? Work with your partner to think of how it might have been included. After you have shared your writing, listen as your partner shares his or her work.*

Share Your Understanding

Invite volunteers to share observations about their opinion writing. Remind them that reflection is different from editing, revising, and peer review. Instead, it is a way to think about our own writing in a new way. Provide the following sentence stems to assist students as they share:

- *This was my first time to write a _____.*
- *I like that I _____.*
- *I wish that I _____.*
- *I especially enjoyed writing _____ because _____.*
- *I didn't really enjoy writing _____ because _____.*

Write a Suggestion

On the bottom of their rubrics, ask students to write a suggestion that would improve one of their opinion pieces. Remind students that suggestions are specific to the writing, focus on an important aspect of the work or the writing process, and are meant to help the writer improve their writing the next time they write.

iELD Integrated ELD

Light Support
Allow students to work with on-level partners to complete the rubric.

Moderate Support
Review the meanings of vocabulary words on the rubric, such as **opinion, reason,** and **closure** as you go through the statements as a group.

Substantial Support
Work one-on-one with students to complete the rubric. Read each statement aloud and help the student locate an example of the skill (or a place where the skill could be used) in his or her opinion writing.

W.1.1 Write opinion pieces in which they introduce the topic or name the book they are writing about, state an opinion, supply a reason for the opinion, and provide some sense of closure. **SL.1.4** Describe people, places, things, and events with relevant details, expressing ideas and feelings clearly.

Reflect on Poetry Writing W.1.5

Engage Thinking

Briefly review the poetry writing assignments students have completed this school year: sensory poems and acrostic poems.

Say: *Now we're going to think about our poetry writing. We'll begin by reviewing the features of poetry writing that we worked on in Unit 10.*

Share the Rubric

Display and read aloud the poetry writing rubric.

Say: *This is a rubric that lists the features and characteristics our poems might have. We're going to use it to help us think about what we did well when we wrote our poems. The rubric can also help us think about ways we could improve our writing.*

Discuss each item on the rubric with the class. Make sure that all your students understand what each element of the rubric describes.

As a poetry writer, I . . .
Choose a title that tells something about the poem's topic.
Follow the required structure of the poetry type.
Use strong, vivid words and phrases.

Poetry Writing Rubric

Reread Poems

Hand out students' poetry portfolios and invite them to reread their work. Distribute copies of the rubric.

Say: *Use the rubric as you read to evaluate your poems. Which poem best fits the rubric? Is that the poem you like the best?*

Have students pick out the poem they think does the best job of including every element in the rubric. Explain to students that they will be sharing this poem with a partner.

Student Objectives

I will be able to:
• Review the features of poetry writing.
• Reflect on my own poetry writing.
• Share my reflections with others.

Additional Materials

• Writing portfolios

Peer Rehearsal (iELD)

Match students with a partner and have each student explain how the poem they selected includes the elements in the rubric.

Say: *Read your poem to your partner. When you are done, point out where you included each of the different elements from the rubric. What if you find there is an element on the rubric that you did not include in your poem? Discuss with your partner whether or not it could be included. Do you both think including it improves your poem? After you have shared your poem, listen as your partner shares his or her poem.*

Share Your Understanding

Invite volunteers to share observations about their poetry writing. Remind them that reflection is different from editing, revising, and peer review. Instead, it is a way to think about our own writing in a new way. Provide the following sentence stems to assist students as they share:

- *This was my first time to write a _____.*
- *I like that I _____.*
- *I wish that I _____.*
- *I especially enjoyed writing _____ because _____.*
- *I didn't really enjoy writing _____ because _____.*

Write a Compliment, Question, or Suggestion

On the bottom of their rubrics, ask students to write a compliment, question, or suggestion about one of their poems.

Remind students about these specific sharing strategies:

- Compliments should be specific to the writing.
- Questions should be about a specific detail of the writing or a part of the writing process. They should focus on an important part of the poem.
- Suggestions should be kind, specific, and focus on helping the writer improve his or her writing next time.

iELD Integrated ELD

Light Support
Allow students to work with on-level partners to complete the rubric.

Moderate Support
Review the meanings of vocabulary words on the rubric, such as **topic, structure,** and **vivid,** as you go through the statements as a group.

Substantial Support
Work one-on-one with students to complete the rubric. Read each statement aloud and help the student locate an example of the skill (or a place where the skill could be used) in his or her poetry writing.

W.1.5 With guidance and support from adults, focus on a topic, respond to questions and suggestions from peers, and add details to strengthen writing as needed.

Share Writing SL.1.4

Engage Thinking

Remind students that they have reviewed the narrative, informational text writing, opinion writing, and poems they've completed this school year and reflected on what they learned about themselves as writers.

Say: *Congratulations on all the great writing you have done and how much your writing has improved. Now you will select one piece of writing to share with the whole class. First, you will tell something about your piece, such as what it means to you or why you chose it. Then you may read aloud your favorite part.*

Let each student pick from all four text types or assign different students to choose a narrative, informational text, opinion text, or poem to make sure all are represented.

Prepare

> **Management Tip:** To better manage class time, you may select samples for each student's work to share prior to the start of class.

Allow students time to look through their portfolios and choose which piece of writing they want to share.

Peer Rehearsal

Have students read their selected writing aloud to a partner, decide what they're going to say about it, and choose their favorite part. Explain that reading through their favorite sentence, paragraph, or section several times will help them become familiar enough with the text to look up occasionally to make eye contact with the audience. Remind students to read at a pace that is clear and understandable and to speak loudly enough to be heard. Monitor and provide feedback as needed. For example:

Directive Feedback: *Slowing down/speeding up your reading will make it easier for listeners to understand and follow.*

Self-Monitoring and Reflection: *Do you think listeners will be able to hear you? Did you remember to change your voice to reflect punctuation marks and meaning?*

Validating and Confirming: *Your voice is at just the right volume, and I like how you read at a faster pace at the exciting part. Keep up the good work!*

Share

Invite students to share their thoughts about their selected piece of writing. Prompt them to explain what makes the piece important to them and then read their favorite sentence, paragraph, or section aloud.

Student Objectives

I will be able to:
• Select a piece of writing to share with the class.

Additional Materials

• Writing portfolios

Celebrate

Have an end-of-year writing celebration to reward students for their work and growth. For example:

- Roll out a red carpet. Have students take turns walking the carpet and receiving an award for one or more aspects of their writing, such as ability to generate ideas, creativity, funny/entertaining style, use of strong adjectives and verbs, editing/revising skills, ability to express and support an opinion, good organizational skills, writing convention skills, use of technology, research skills, willingness to help others, noteworthy effort, and most improved.
- Watch a slide show of writing class photographs from the school year.
- Present each student with a notebook to use as a summer journal. Allow time for students to autograph one another's journals.
- Have snacks!

Closure (End of Year)

To wrap up the school year:

- Retain any writing samples needed to meet your school's ongoing documentation requirements.
- Invite each student to contribute one piece of writing to a class book for next year's students to read.
- Allow students to take the rest of their writing home. Encourage them to share their work with their families.

Integrated ELD

Light Support
Pair students with a more fluent partner for Peer Rehearsal.

Moderate Support
Offer a recording of a fluent reading of students' chosen excerpts, encouraging them to practice reading along with it to improve pronunciation, phrasing, and expression.

Substantial Support
In addition to multiple readings with a partner, provide extra modeling and practice with oral reading to help students gain confidence and fluency.

SL.1.4 Describe people, places, things, and events with relevant details, expressing ideas and feelings clearly.

Blackline Masters

BLM 1 Write Opinion Text: State an Opinion 144

BLM 2 Write Opinion Text: Draft 145

BLM 3 Write Opinion Text: Revise and Edit 146

BLM 4 Write Informational Text: Brainstorm 147

BLM 5 Write Informational Text: Brainstorm 148

BLM 6 Write Informational Text: Plan 149

BLM 7 Write Informational Text: Plan 150

BLM 8 Write Informational Text: Draft 151

BLM 9 Write Informational Text: Revise and Edit 152

BLM 10 Write Informational Text: Revise and Edit 153

BLM 11 Write a Narrative: Brainstorm 154

BLM 12 Write a Narrative: Brainstorm 155

BLM 13 Write a Narrative: Plan 156

BLM 14 Write a Narrative: Plan 157

BLM 15 Write a Narrative: Draft 158

BLM 16 Write a Narrative: Revise and Edit 159

BLM 17 Write a Narrative: Revise and Edit 160

BLM 18 Write Opinion Text: State an Opinion 161

BLM 19 Write Opinion Text: Plan 162

BLM 20 Write Opinion Text: Plan 163

BLM 21 Write Opinion Text: Revise and Edit 164

BLM 22 Read a Personal Narrative Mentor Text 165

BLM 23 Personal Narrative: Brainstorm 166

BLM 24 Personal Narrative: Planning 167

BLM 25 Personal Narrative: Writing a Draft 168

BLM 26 Personal Narrative: Add a Conclusion 169

BLM 27 Personal Narrative: Revise to Add Time Words 170

BLM 28 Personal Narrative: Revise to Add Descriptive Details . 171

BLM 29 Personal Narrative: Edit for Capitalization 172

BLM 30 Publish the Personal Narrative 173

BLM 31 Read an Informational Mentor Text 174

BLM 32 Informational Text: Brainstorm 175

BLM 33 Informational Text: Planning 176

BLM 34 Informational Text: Planning **177**

BLM 35 Informational Text: Writing a Draft **178**

BLM 36 Informational Text: Write a Title and a Conclusion . . **179**

BLM 37 Informational Text: Revise to Add More Facts **180**

BLM 38 Informational Text: Revise to Add Visual Support . . . **181**

BLM 39 Informational Text: Revise to Add Visual Support . . . **182**

BLM 40 Informational Text: Edit the Draft to Correct
Spelling Errors. **183**

BLM 41 Publish the Informational Text **184**

BLM 42 Publish the Informational Text **185**

BLM 43 Opinion Text: Brainstorm **186**

BLM 44 Opinion Text: Planning **187**

BLM 45 Opinion Text: Planning **188**

BLM 46 Opinion Text: Edit for End Punctuation **189**

BLM 47 Publish the Opinion Text **190**

BLM 48 Informational Report:
Analyze a Prompt and Read a Mentor Text **191**

BLM 49 Informational Report: Find Details in Text Sources. . . **192**

BLM 50 Informational Report: Find Facts in Media Sources . . **193**

BLM 51 Informational Report: Planning **194**

BLM 52 Informational Report: Revise to Add a
Conclusion and a Title **195**

BLM 53 Informational Report: Publish Report **196**

Name _____ Date _____

Opinion Chart

Characters	I like this character because...

Name _____ Date _____

Singular and Plural Nouns and Matching Verbs Chart

The Gingerbread Man _____ through the countryside.
The two animals _____ the Gingerbread Man.
The fox _____.

Name _____ Date _____

Editing Checklist

Editing	Check
I used pronouns correctly.	
I used correct end punctuation for each sentence.	
I used singular and plural nouns with matching verbs.	
I used the correct articles where they were needed.	
I spelled all words correctly.	
I capitalized the first letter of the first word in each sentence.	

Name _____ Date _____

Brainstorming Chart

Plants	Animals

Name _____ Date _____

Pronouns Chart

Pronouns	Sentences
Their	The ducks made fun of the ugly duckling. _____ made fun of him.
He	The ducks followed the mother duck. _____ mother kept them safe.
They	The ugly duckling was alone. _____ felt lonely.

Name _____ Date _____

Planning Chart

Stages in the Life Cycle	Facts

Name _____ Date _____

Personal Pronouns Chart

Pronouns	Sentences
He	The ugly duckling was sad about what happened to **the ugly duckling.**
Him	**The ugly duckling** told what happened to the ugly duckling.
His	**The ugly duckling's** family abandoned him.

Name _____ Date _____

Singular and Plural Nouns with Matching Verbs

Singular Noun and Verb	Plural Noun and Verb
The duck swims.	
The egg cracks.	
The swan talks.	

Name _____ Date _____

Editing Checklist

Editing	Check
I used pronouns correctly.	
I used correct end punctuation for each sentence.	
I used singular and plural nouns with matching verbs.	
I spelled all words correctly.	
I capitalized the first letter of the first word in each sentence.	

Name _____ Date _____

Singular and Plural Nouns with Matching Verbs Chart

Sentences Without a Verb	Sentences With a Verb
Mother duck (lead/leads) her ducklings.	
The ducklings (tease/teases) the ugly duckling.	
The swans (is/are) nice to the ugly duckling.	

Name _____ Date _____

Brainstorming Chart

Characters	Setting	Events

Name _____ Date _____

Commas Chart

Sentences Without Commas	Sentences With Commas
Fox was crafty sly and tricky.	
Little Red Hen was smart patient and brave.	
Fox felt hot tired and sweaty on the way home.	

Name _____ Date _____

Planning Chart

Big Ideas	Details

Name _____ Date _____

Commas Chart

Sentences/Dates Without Commas	Sentences/Dates With Commas
Little Red Hen is smart brave and clever.	
Mother Fox is patient caring and loving.	
January 1 2018	

Name _____ Date _____

Adjectives Chart

Character	Adjectives
Little Red Hen	
Fox	
Mother Fox	

Name _____ Date _____

Editing Checklist

Editing	Check
I used adjectives in my descriptions.	
I used correct end punctuation for each sentence.	
I used commas correctly.	
I spelled all words correctly.	
I capitalized the first letter of the first word in each sentence.	

Name _____ Date _____

Adjectives Chart

Sentences	Adjectives
The _____ fox tries to trick Little Red Hen.	
Little Red Hen put a _____ in the bag.	
Little Red Hen lived in a _____ house near the woods.	

Name _____ Date _____

Brainstorming Chart

Using Technology at Work	Technology Breakdown

Name _____ Date _____

Planning Chart

Part of Writing	Details

Name _____ Date _____

Prepositions Chart

When	Where

Name _____ Date _____

Editing Checklist

Editing	Check
I used correct end punctuation for each type of sentence.	
I used prepositions correctly.	
I spelled all words correctly.	
I capitalized the first letter of the first word in each sentence.	

Name _____ Date _____

Conjunctions Chart

Turtle is lazy. Turtle is selfish.	
The geese warn Turtle. He keeps talking.	
Turtle can eat the apple. Turtle can eat the pear.	
Turtle's shell cracks. He falls on some rocks.	

Name _____ Date _____

Conjunctions Chart

The animals held a meeting _____ they could talk about Turtle.

Turtle could have been quiet, _____ he kept talking.

Turtle promised not to be greedy, _____ he got his own food.

Turtle's shell cracked _____ he landed on some rocks.

Do you think Turtle will be lazy _____ selfish anymore?

Name _____ Date _____

Sequence of Events Chart

Beginning

Middle

End

Name _____ Date _____

Conjunctions Chart

The animals are upset with Turtle because _____.
Turtle goes with the geese, so _____.
Turtle cries because _____.
In the story, Turtle acts badly, but _____.

Name _____ Date _____

Conjunctions Chart

The Great Turtle Leader is proud of his shell _____.
Animals bring Turtle food _____.
The animals grow tired of Turtle's _____.
Things change when winter approaches, _____.

Name _____ Date _____

Conjunctions Chart

Mosquito talks about huge yams, _____ Iguana does not believe him.

Iguana doesn't want to hear Mosquito, _____ she puts sticks in her ears.

Python hides in a hole _____ he thinks Iguana is angry with him.

Name _____ Date _____

Conjunctions Chart

Rabbit hops through the forest because _____.
Monkey wants to warn the animals, so _____.
Lion King calls all the animals to a meeting, but _____.
Mosquito can come out and speak, or _____.
Mother Owl finds her baby, and _____.

Name _____ Date _____

Sentences Chart

Kind of Sentence	What It Does	End Mark	Sample Sentences
Declarative			
Imperative			
Interrogative			
Exclamatory			

Name _____ Date _____

Publishing Checklist

Feature	Digital Publication	Handwritten
title at top		
author's name under title		
darker font for title and author		
clear handwriting		
correct spacing		
add a drawing (optional)		

Name _____ Date _____

Nouns and Matching Verbs Chart

Unmatched Nouns and Verbs	Matched Nouns and Verbs
The girl help.	
The boys sings.	
My uncle walk to work.	
The children plays soccer.	

Name _____ Date _____

Nouns and Matching Verbs Chart

Singular Nouns and Matching Verbs	Plural Nouns and Matching Verbs
student eats	
teacher tells	
ball bounces	
dog runs	

Name _____ Date _____

Informational Text Planning Chart

Topic:	
Key Ideas	**Facts**

Name _____ Date _____

Nouns and Matching Verbs Chart

Singular Nouns and Matching Verbs	Plural Nouns and Matching Verbs
diagram shows	
computer helps	
artist illustrates	
time line shows	

Name _____ Date _____

Nouns and Matching Verb Chart

Sentence Frame	Verbs	Completed Sentence
The Native Americans _____ hard.	work/works	
A dentist _____ my teeth.	clean/cleans	
The Taj Mahal _____ nice.	look/looks	
The parrots _____ loudly.	whistle/whistles	

Name _____ Date _____

Nouns and Matching Verbs Chart

Incorrect Sentence	Correct Sentence
The schools opens at 8:00.	
The glass fall on the floor.	
A duck quack loudly.	
A dog catch the ball.	

Name _____ Date _____

Matching Nouns and Verbs Chart

Singular Nouns and Verbs	Plural Nouns and Verbs
The boy visits the monument.	
The memorial has a lot of visitors.	
The building is famous.	
The citizen works hard.	

Name _____ Date _____

Visual Support Planning Chart

Text	Image

Name _____ Date _____

Nouns and Matching Verb Chart

Singular Nouns and Matching Verbs	Plural Nouns and Matching Verbs
The girl visits the memorial.	
The memorial honors the president.	
The worker carves the memorial.	
The boy walks to school.	

Name _____ Date _____

Possessive Nouns Chart

Nouns	Possessive Nouns
boy jacket	
girl hat	
baby toy	
Mom car	
Dad bike	

Name _____ Date _____

Publishing Checklist

Feature	Computer	Handwritten
title at top		
author's name under title		
special font for title and author		
clear handwriting		
correct spacing		
supporting images (optional)		

Name _____ Date _____

Possessive Nouns Chart

Nouns	Possessive Nouns
teachers	
class	
babies	
mothers	
bus	

Name _____ Date _____

Opinion Chart

Topic	Opinion

Name _____ Date _____

Opinion Chart

Topic	Opinion	Reason

Name _____ Date _____

Verb Tense Chart

Present Tense Verbs	Past Tense Verbs
I look at the moon at night.	I looked at the moon last night.
John protects his eyes from the sun.	John protected his eyes from the sun yesterday.
We count the stars in the sky.	We counted the stars in the sky last night.

Name _____ Date _____

Pronoun Chart

Sentence	Type of Pronoun
We can see stars in the night sky.	
One reason stars are interesting is because **they** form pictures.	
Karla looked through **her** telescope.	
She saw **something** race through the night sky.	

Name _____ Date _____

Publishing Checklist

Feature	Digital Publication	Handwritten
title at top		
author's name under title		
darker font for title and author		
clear handwriting		
correct spacing		

Name _____ Date _____

Adjectives Chart

Original Sentence	Question	New Sentence with an Adjective
Bill lives in a house.	What kind of house?	
We bought coats.	What kind of coats?	
The car was parked by the curb.	What kind of car?	
The garden was full of flowers.	What kind of flowers?	

Name _____ Date _____

Notetaking Chart

Source:	Notes

Name _____ Date _____

Adjective Chart

Noun	Adjectives
Father	
Mother	
Children	
Food	

Name _____ Date _____

Informational Report Planning Chart

Topic:	
Key Ideas	**Facts**

Name _____ Date _____

Commas in Dates Chart

Nouns
July 17 2011
Wednesday April 6
Wednesday April 6 2016

Name _____ Date _____

Publishing Checklist

Feature	Computer	Handwritten
title at top		
author's name under title		
special font for title and author		
clear handwriting		
correct spacing		
supporting images (optional)		

Notes

Notes